Pitseolak: Pictures out of my life

ᐱᓯᐅᓚᒃ: ᐅᓂᑲᑐᐊᒃ ᐃᓄᓯᐅᓚᐅ'ᑐᒥᒃ

© Dorothy Eber, 1971
First paperback edition, 1978
ISBN-0-295-95632-1
Library of Congress catalog card number: 72-4111

Design:
Rolf Harder and Ernst Roch
Printing:
Gazette Canadian Printing Ltd.
Typesetting:
Metro Typesetters Inc. (English)
Department of Indian Affairs and Northern Development (Eskimo)
Printed in Canada

The drawing 'A bird for the doctor' is reproduced with the kind
permission of Dr. and Mrs. Samuel Adams.

Pitseolak:
Pictures out of my life

From recorded interviews by Dorothy Eber

University of Washington Press, Seattle

Acknowledgments

The publishers wish to express their appreciation and
thanks to
The Department of Indian Affairs and Northern Development for provision of the Eskimo text,
The Canada Council for a grant to assist with the tape-
recording,
The West Baffin Eskimo Co-operative for its loan of stone
cuts, engravings and original drawings,
The National Museum of Man for its loan of stone cuts and
engravings,
Mrs. Alma Houston for advice and encouragement.

ᑲᐅᕆᑎᒍᔪᑎ

ᑕᑯᐊ ᐊᑐᐊᑕᓕᐳᑐᒃ ᐃᓄᑲᑎᐹᑯᓂ ᐊᑯᒥᒍᒪᔪ ᐃᓄ
ᐱᓇᕐᐊᑎᕐᒃ ᐃᓄᑐᒃᓕᑎᕐᓕᐳᒪᓕᑎ ᑕᕐᒥᓕ,
ᐊᓕᓗ ᐊᕐᕆᕐᑦ ᓂᐱᓕᐳᓂᔪᑦ ᐃᑲᕐᓕᐳᑐ,
ᑲᕐᐊᓕᕐᐳᓗ ᑯᐳᐊᐸᑕ ᑎᑎᑐᕐᓕᒃᐳᑐᓕᑎᕐᓂᕐᒃ ᐊᑐᑎᕐᓕᐳᑐᒃ,
ᑲᓂᑕ ᕐ ᓄᑕᐳᕐᑐᓂ ᑭᕐᐹᕐᒃ ᑎᑎᑐᕐᓕᒃᐳᑐᓕᑎᕐᓂᕐᒃ
ᐊᑐᑎᕐᓕᐳᑐᒃ,
ᐊᓕᓗ ᐊᕐᒪ ᕐᓕᑕᕐ ᐃᓕᐃᓕᑐᕐᕐᐊ ᑲᓗᓕ ᐱᑯᐹᓕᓗᓄ,
ᑕᑯᐊ ᐃᓄᐊᑎᕐᒃ ᐊᕐᕐᐊᓗ ᐊᑐᕐᑕᐳᕐᓕᑦ.

Travelling by sleigh (detail).
Coloured pencil and felt pen,
ca. 1967

ᑭᒍᓯᑐᑦ (ᐃᒪᐃᓕᓚᓂᓚ)
ᑕᒃᓴᓕᖕᑦ ᐊᒪᓗ ᐃᒪᓕᖕᑦ ᐊᓚᐅᑎᖕᑦ
ᑎᑎᑐᓚ, 1967 ᐅᑎᓗᒍ

Foreword

It is mid-July, 1970, and brilliant Arctic summer, when I ask Pitseolak if I may tape her autobiography. I have come to Cape Dorset on Baffin Island especially for the purpose and, very soon after the Nordair Otter touches down, I go looking for Quatsia Ottochie. Quatsia, nineteen and a modern Eskimo beauty, knows at firsthand the story of the Cape Dorset art movement. Her father, Ottochie (whose name she has adopted now that Eskimos need surnames), has worked in the craft shop of the West Baffin Eskimo Co-operative since shortly after print-making began, in the late fifties. Her English has been perfected by a typing course in the south, and she agrees to interpret and help put my proposition to Pitseolak. So, with tape recorder, a big bag of tapes, notebooks and coloured pens and drawing paper, we present ourselves at Pitseolak's house. At the beginning of the sixties most Baffin Island Eskimos still lived on the land in igloos and skin tents but now, like Pitseolak, they live in clapboard bungalows.

ᑲᐅᔨᑎᓯᐅᑎᒋᑦ

ᔭᓗ ᑕᑭᓚᓂ, 1970-ᒥ ᐊᒪᓗ ᑲᐅᒪᔭᐸᓗᑎᓗᒍ ᐃᖕᐃᑦ ᖕᓇᓚ ᐊᐅᔭᑯ, ᐊᐱᓯᓚᐅᔭᔭᓚ ᐱᓯᐅᓚᒥ ᓂᐱᓕᐅᕈᓇᒪᓚᒪ ᐅᓂᑲᐅᓯᓕᐊᓚᓂ. ᑭᓚᖕᓚᐅᑐᓚ ᐃᖕᐃ ᖕᓇᓚᖕ ᑕᓯᒥᓚᓗᐊᒍᐊ ᒍᑎᑲᓯᓚ; ᐊᒪᓗ ᑲᓚᑕᓯ ᑐᒋᕋᒍᑐᐊᒪ, ᒥᕕᒧ ᑕᓇ ᐃᖕᐃ ᒪᓂᑲᓴᑕᕕᓂᓚ ᖕᓇᒥ ᒪᓂᕋᒥ ᑲᑲᐃᑦ ᐅᓚᑕᓂ ᖕᓇᓕᓂᑦ ᒪᑐᐃᒪᔭᓂ, ᑭᓂᓯᓚᐅᑐᓚ ᑯᐊᓯᐊ ᐅᒃᑐᑭᒥ. ᑯᐊᓯᐊ 19-ᓂ ᐅᑭᐅᑲᑐᒃ ᐊᒃᓇᓯᐊᕙᐅᓗᓂ, ᑲᐅᔨᒪᓴᐅᑎᒋᓚᐅᑐ ᓯᕗᓕᒥ ᐅᓂᑲᑐᐊᓚᓂ ᑭᓚᐃᑦ ᓴᓇᒍᐊᑲᑕᓂᒋᓂ. ᑯᐊᓯᐊᑉ ᐊᑕᑕᓚ, ᐅᒃᑐᑭ (ᑕᓯᒪ ᐊᑎᓚ ᑯᐊᓯᐊᑉ ᑎᒍᐊᒍᓚᒥ ᒪᓇ ᐃᖕᐃᑦ ᐊᑎᑲᑎᐊᑲᒪᑕ), ᐃᑲᓇᐃᔭᓯᒪᓕᑐ ᓴᓇᒍᐊᓯᒪᔭᑯᕕᒥ ᐃᖕᐃᑦ ᖕᓇᓚᑕ ᑯᐅᐊᐸᓚᓂ ᐱᒋᐊᓯᕋᑕᑎᓗᒋᑦ ᑎᑎᑐᔭᓕᐅᓯᔭᕕᓂᒃ, ᐊᕋᒍᐃ 1950 ᐱᒋᐊᓯᒪᓕᑎᓗᒥ. ᑯᐊᓯᐊ ᑲᓗᓇᑎᑐᓯᐊᕈᓇᓚ ᐅᑐᒃ ᐃᓕᓂᐊᓯᒪᓚᒥ ᑎᑎᕋᐅᑎᒥ ᓇᑭᑕᑐᒥ ᑲᓗᓇᑦ ᖕᓇᓚᓂ, ᐊᒪᓗ ᐊᒋᓚᐅᑐ ᑐᓴᔪᐅᒋᐊᓴᒥᓂ ᐃᑲᔭᓗᓂ ᐅᑲᐅᓯᑎᔭᒪᔭᓂ ᐱᓯᐅᓚᒍ. ᑕᐃᒪ ᓂᐱᓕᐅᕈᑎᐅᑉ ᓂᐱᓴᒋᓂ ᐃᐱᐊᔭ ᑕᑕᓗᒍ, ᐊᒪᓗ ᑎᑎᑐᔭᕕᓴᓂ ᐊᔪᒋᒋᑐᓂᓗ ᑎᑎᕋᐅᑎᓂ ᐊᒪᓗ ᐸᐃᐸᓂ ᑎᑎᑐᔭᕕᓴᓂ ᓇᔭᓯᓯᖕ ᐃᑎᓕᓚᐅᑐᒍ ᐱᓯᐅᓚᑉ ᐃᒃᓗᓚᖕ. ᐱᒋᐊᓚᑕᑎᓗᒋ ᐊᕋᒍᐃ 1960 ᐃᓗᓇᑲᓴᑎ ᐃᖕᐃ ᖕᓇᓚᓂᒥᐅ

Bird.
Stone cut, 1967

ᑯᐸᓄᐊᒃ
ᐅᔭᕋᒥ ᑎᑎᑐᒐ, I967

Pitseolak and I have met two years earlier and, with the help of Quatsia, we exchange greetings. Quatsia and I take off our rubber boots and walk into Pitseolak's warm kitchen. Quickly I realize that since our first meeting "acculturation", as the sociologists say, has proceeded at a speedy clip. Then, Pitseolak sat on the floor and drew as we talked; now she sits on a couch, there is a telephone on the wall and across the room is a bowl of plastic flowers. But there is soon no doubt that Pitseolak herself is the same: wise, humorous, a sage commentator on the sociology of change and, of course, the possessor of a remarkable talent which allows her to draw as many as six pictures a morning of vivid interest and beauty.

After preliminaries, Quatsia explains there are people in the south who would like to make a book with some of Pitseolak's drawings and prints and her life story, told in her own words. There is brisk talk back and forth and then Quatsia says, "She doesn't mind to do it but she is getting old now. She is getting kind of shaky and the drawings

ᓯᓕ ᓄᓇᒥᓚᐅᑐ ᐃᒃ ᓗᕕᒐᒥᓯᑎ ᑭᓯᓂᓗ ᑐᐱᑲᓯᑎ ᒪᓇᓕ, ᐱᓯᐅᓚᑎᑐᑦ, ᐃᒃ ᓗᑐᐃᓇᒥ ᐃᒃ ᓗᑲᓕᑐᑦ.

ᐱᓯᐅᓚᓗ ᑲᑎᒋᐅᓚᐅᓯᒪᔪᒧ ᐅᑭᐅ ᒪᕈ ᓇᓯᒪᓕᑐᒃ ᐊᒪᓗ, ᐃᑲᔪᑎᑲᒥᓯᒐᑕᐅᒃ ᑯᐊᓯᐊᒥᒃ, ᐅᑲᑲᑎᒋᓯᑕ. ᑯᐊᓯᐊᓗ ᑲᒥᓚᓯᓄ ᓂᑭᓕᐅᕕᒐᓄ ᐅᑯᔪᒧ ᐃᑎᑐᒧ. ᑲᐅᕗᓴᐅᑎᒋᐊᐱᑐᒐ ᑕᐃᒪᒪᒐᓂ ᑲᑎᓚᐅᓯᒪᒪᒐᑯ ᓯᕗᓕᒥ "ᐃᓄᐃ ᐃᓄᓯᑐᑲᕕᓂᒐᓂᒃ" ᑲᐅᕗᓴᑎᒃ ᐅᑲᐅᓯᑎᓯᒪᔭᒐᑎᑐ, ᓯᑲᑐᐸᓗᒥ ᐊᕗᐅᒋᓕᓯᒪᔪ. ᑕᐃᒪ ᐱᓯᐅᓚ ᐃᓯᕙᓗᓂ ᓇᑎᒥ ᑎᑎᑐᔭᓯᓯᓂᓗ ᐅᑲᑎᓗᑕ; ᒪᓇᓕ ᐃᓯᕙᐅᑕᓗᒥ ᐃᓯᕙᓕᑐ, ᐅᑲᓚᐅᑎ ᐊᑭᓇᒥᓗᓂ ᐊᒪᓗ ᐃᒃ ᓗᒧᓯᐅ ᑐᑭᐊᓂ ᐳᒧᑕ ᓄᓇᒧᐊᑕᑲᓗᓂ. ᐃᓚ ᓯᐊᕈᓕᒪ ᓇᓗᓇᒋᑐᒃ ᐱᓯᐅᓚ ᑕᓇᓴᐃᓇᐅᒋᐊᒐ: ᓯᓚᑐᓗᓂ, ᑯᕕᐊᓯᑐᐃ ᓇᓗᓂ, ᐃᓯᒪᓯᐊᓗᓂ, ᑲᐅᕗᒪᓯᐊᑐ ᐃᓄᐃᑦ ᓄᓇᒐᑕ ᐊᕗᐅᒋ ᓕᓂᒐᓂᒃ ᐊᒪᓗ, ᓯᑲᐃᒪ ᐊᑭᓯᐃᕗᒃ, ᐊᔪᒋᓂᒥᓄᑦ ᑕᐃᒪᓇ ᑎᑎᑐᔭᓗᓂ ᐅᓄᓂᑲᑐᓂᒃ ᐱᒐᓯᔪᑐᓂ ᐊᕗᒧᐊᓕᐅᓗᓂ ᐅᒃᓚᑯ ᐃᓄᓯᓚᑎᑎᑐᑦ ᐱᐅᔪᐸᓗᓂᒃ ᐃᓇᑯᓇᓗᑎᓗ.

ᐅᑲᑲᑎᒋᓚᐅᓯᑕ ᑲᓄᐃᓂᒋᓂᐊᑕᑎᓂ ᑯᐊᓯᐊ ᑐᑭᓯᑎᓯᓯᐊᓚᐅᑐ ᑲᓗᓇᑦ ᓄᓇᒐᓂᑐᓂᒃ ᓴᓇᔪᑲᒧᒪᒪᑦ ᐅᓂᑲᑐᐊᒥᒃ ᐱᓯᐅᓚᑉ ᑎᑎᑐᔭᑕᕕᓂᒋᓂᒃ ᐊᒪᓗ ᐃᓄᓯᒐᑕ ᐅᓂᑲᐅᓯᒐᓂ, ᐅᑲᓯᒪᔪᓂ

Joyful owl.
Stone cut, 1961

ᗪᐱᐊᑉᒧᑊ ᐅᑊ ᐱᑊ
ᐅᐸᑕᒥ ᑎᑎᖑᒪ, I96I

are sometimes shaky. And she doesn't remember everything though she remembers many things.''

All is arranged. For the next three weeks I spend nearly
every afternoon at Pitseolak's house. There are frequent
interruptions to these taping sessions. There are telephone calls, and Pitseolak's grown-up children and her
grandchildren often come in to listen or to visit. One day
a son brings ice cream tubs, the greatest treat of the year.
They have arrived that day on the long awaited sea-lift.
He also brings molasses which Pitseolak says is to put in
the tea. ''I used to like it in the camps and I still like it,''
she says. All conversation stops while these good things
are relished.

Each day, when I arrive, Pitseolak brings out a large
sketch book and we look at the drawings she has done
in the morning — they are rarely shaky and always they
show Pitseolak's distinctive line and style. Then we
move on to reminiscences. Pitseolak's memories do not

ᗩᒥᓂ ᐅᑉᐅᒡᒥᓂ ᐊᒧᓄ. ᒡᑉᒍᒥ ᐅᑉᑫᑎᒧᑉᓴᓂ ᑕᐃᒪ
ᕗᐊᒉᐊᑊ ᐅᑉᓴᓂ "ᑕᓄ ᑫᓂᐃᕿᒦᑊ ᐅᓂᑉᐅᕑᐅᖑᐊᒍᓂ
ᕿᒉᓂᒍ ᒪᓇ ᓂᕒᐅᒉᐸᖕᐊᑫᒧᑊ. ᕼᐊᒍᒉᐊᖕᓂᓄᓗ
ᑎᑎᖕᒉᑎ ᐃᓴᖑᑯ ᕼᐊᖑᑯᒍᑎ. ᐊᒪᓗ ᐊᐅᒉᕑᒧᒧᐊᑊ
ᐃᓴᓂᕒᐃᑊ ᐊᒦᕑᐃᑊ ᐊᐅᒉᕑᒪᓗᐊᒥᖕ".

ᐃᓴᓂᕒ ᐊᑉᕑᒉᒧᑎ. ᐱᓂᕑᐊᕑᕒᐃᓂ ᐱᒦᒥᖕ ᕿᓐᒋᑎᐊᑕᒉᕑ
ᐱᕑᐅᑊ ᐊᕒᒡᒧᑊᑕᑫᐅᒪ. ᖟᑊᓐᕒᕼᑊᑫᓐᒍ ᑕᖟᒧᒪ
ᓂᕿᑎᐅᓐᒍᑊ. ᐅᑫᑎᐅᒧ ᕒᕿᖟᑊᑫᒧᓂ, ᐊᒪᓗ ᐱᕑᐅᑊ
ᕿᒍᒉᕑᑊ ᐃᓂᐅᑎᐊᑊ ᐊᒍᒦᕒᒧ ᐊᑎᕿᖑᑊ ᖟᒦᕑᐊᒍᕑᓐᑊ
ᕒᑫᓐᐊᖟᓐᒧᒍ. ᐊᑊᐅᕑᐊᕒᓂ ᐃᑊᖟᒥ ᑎᕿᐅᕒᑫᐅᕑᕒ ᐊᒍᖕᒦ
ᕼᐊᖑᑊ, ᑕᓇ ᐊᕒᓂᕒᒦᑊ ᐱᒪᖟᕒᐊᑊ ᐊᒡᒍᕒ. ᑕᒡᐊ
ᑎᕿᒉᑊᑊ ᑕᐃᕒᒪᒧᐊᑎᒧᒍ ᐊᒡᓂ ᐅᑊᕿᑊᒉᕒᑎ ᕒᒡᕒᓂᒪᓂ.
ᐊᒪᑫᐅ ᑕᓇ ᐃᑊᖟᒥ ᑎᕿᐅᕒᑫᐅᕒᕒᒦᑊ ᒪᑕᕼᒦᕒ ᐱᕑᐅᑊ
ᐅᑊᒧᒥ ᑎᒍᒍᑊ ᐃᑎᒦᒪ. "ᒪᒪᑎᕼᑫᐅᕒᐅᕒᑊ ᓄᐊᓄᕒᑕ ᕒᑎ
ᒪᒪᑎᕼᕒᑊ". ᐅᑊᒧᒥ ᐱᕑᐅᑊ. ᐃᑊ ᓄᐊᑎ ᐅᑊᑫᑎᑎᒍ ᖟᑊᓄᒍ
ᑕᒡᐊ ᒪᒪᒍᐃᑊ ᓂᕒᕼᐅᒦᕒᓂ.

ᑫᐅᑕᒦᕒ, ᑎᕿᑫᒪ, ᐱᕑᐅᑊ ᓄᐊᕒᒧᒥ ᐊᕒᓂᒥ ᑎᑎᖟᕼᐊᕿᖕ
ᕿᒦᕑᒧᑕᒧ ᑎᑎᖟᕒᒉᒪᕒᓂ ᐱᕑᐅᑊ ᑎᑎᖟᑕᖟᓂᕒᓂ ᐅᑕᒍ--

usually concern the hunt or the harsh times many Eskimos experienced in the old days. Many of the hours we spend together are 'how-to' sessions – how to sew a sealskin tent, how to make mukluks, how to catch a goose without a weapon. She also speaks of domestic felicity and home-life in the camps. In fact, when Pitseolak speaks of difficulties, they are usually the ones the new times have brought along. Like people of the older generations all over the world, she often worries about her grandchildren and whether they can make their way in today's world.

But Pitseolak's story is also an account of how Cape Dorset, a remote point on the Hudson Strait, became an internationally recognized artists' colony. (Today there is hardly a European or North American public art gallery without a Dorset graphic.) Pitseolak makes mention of many of the Dorset artists; and she also speaks with great affection of two white men: the almost legendary James Houston, now an executive with Steuben Glass, New York, who during the fifties was the first civil administrator for

ᔕᔭᐂᐊᓂᐅᐅᐸᐸᐊᑐ ᑕᐅᒪᒪᒪᒪᓗ ᑕᖕᓵᐅᓴᐣ ᐱᔪᐅᑉᑕ ᐣᓐᐳ ᖕᓐᐳᓂᓗᑕᓐ
ᑐᑭᒍᐊᓱ ᐸᐹᓗᓂᓗᐦᓄᓗ. ᑕᒪᓕ ᐊᖕᐅᓕᔭᖕ ᐱᕐᐊᓂᔭᓄᑕ(.
ᐱᔪᐅᑎ ᐊᐅᖕᑕᐅᔪᕗ ᐊᒋᓖᖕᖕ<ᔕᖕ ᐅᓕᔭᐱᐅᒪᖕ ᐅᖁᓄ
ᐊᖕᐅᒋᔪᑕᐅᔭᐃᓇᓄ ᐊᖕ ᐊᓄᐊᓐ ᐅᑐᓕᔕᓄ ᐅᖕᔭᐸ
ᓗᐅᑐ. ᐊᖕᓄ ᐊᖕᐅᓂ ᑲᐣᒪᒍᐣᕈᐅᑕᐳ ᑲᓴ ᐅᖕᐦᓂᑕᑕᑕ
ᖕᓄᐊᒍᒪᒪᓐ(, ᖕᓄᔑ ᖕᓮᐦᒍᒪᒪᓐ(ᓴᕀᐸᖕ ᑭᒦᓄ ᐅᐊᖕᖕ
ᖕᓄᔑ ᖕᖕᑕᐅᕐᒍᒪᒪᓐ(ᖕᓄᔑ ᓂᖕ ᓮᕐᒍᒪᒪᓐ(ᑯᐳᐊᐅᑐᐅᔕᑐ.
ᐱᔪᐅᑎ ᐅᖕᐅᖕᖕᓄᐅᐅᔭᖕ ᐊᓐ ᓕᒪ ᐣᕀᐊᓐᕀᖕᕀᖕ ᐊᒪᔑ
ᐊᖕᖕᑐᖕᓂᐅᓂ ᐊᓇᕐᓕᖕ ᖕᓄᕐᐅᓐ(. ᐊᑐᓐᒋᒪᑐ, ᐱᔪᐅᖕᖕ
ᐅᖕᐅᕀᖕᑕᐅᕐᒍᒪᖕ ᐊᖕᐅᒋᒍᑕᐅᔕᓄ, ᑕᑯᐊᒍᖕᑐ ᓚᐅᐅᓂᒪ
ᐊᒍᓄᑐᒪ. ᑕᑯᐊᓐᑐ ᐊᓄᐊᓐ ᐊᓲᖕᐅᖕᒪᕐᑐ ᓂᕀᔕᓗᐊᓄ
ᕀᑯᕙᐊᒪ, ᐱᔪᐅᑎ ᐊᓄᖕᒍᖕ ᐊᒋᓗᖕᕀᖕᖕ(ᖕᐅᐅᑐ ᑭᐅᓗᕀᑕᑕ
ᒦᖕᓄ ᐊᒪᖕ ᐁᖕ ᒍᑕᕐᑕᐊ ᒦᖕᓄ ᐱᔭᖕᕀᓄᐊᒪᒪᓄᖕᓂᑕᓄ ᐊᐅᔭᕐᒪ
ᓚᐅᐊᑐᐅᔕᕀᑭᐅᕀᔕᓄ.

ᐊᓄ ᐱᔪᐅᑎ ᐅᖕᐊᖕᑕᒍ ᐅᖕᐊᕀᖕᕀᖕᑕᐅᕐᕀᑕᑕᖕᖕᐅᑭ ᐱᖕᐊ
ᖕᓄᐊᖕᓗᓂ, ᑕᑕᒐᓗᖕᔕᓂᑐ ᐊᓄᐊ ᓄᐊᓐᓗᓂ Hudson Strait
ᒪ, ᑕᕀᓄᒦᐅᒍᔭᕐᓄᓐᑕ ᐣᐣᓄᒐᕀᓐᒋ ᓄᐊᒦ. (ᓚᒪ ᐱᑕᕀᑕᕀᔕᓄ
ᑐᖕ ᐅᐲᐣᐱᒦᕀᐅᓂᖕᕀ ᐅᖕᐅᐊᓄ ᐊᒋᔑᐣᕀᓄᑕᐊᖕ ᓄᐊᓗ(ᑕᒐᓗᓄ
ᓄᐊᑕᕀ ᔑᐅᕐᓗᕀᑕᕀᕀᖕ ᕀᒦᐅᑕᕀᐊᓄᓂ ᐱᑕᕀᓇᒍ ᕀᓕᕐᐅᑕᕀ ᐣᐣ

Ancient stone dwelling.
Stone cut, 1966

ᐅᕙᓯᐊᑐᐊᖅ ᐃᓄᒡᕆᖅᐸᑐᐱᓄᖅ
ᐅᖅᖓᒥ ᑎᑎᑐᒪ, 1966

West Baffin Island; and Terrence Ryan, art director of the West Baffin Eskimo Co-operative.

Both have played major roles in the Cape Dorset story. It was James Houston who first encouraged Eskimos to send their carving south. They have a centuries-old tradition of craftsmanship in stone and bone; and in the nineteenth century they sold many small ivory carvings, often with incised drawings, to the crews of the whaling ships. Houston first saw their carvings in the late forties on a sketching trip he made to the North. He brought back examples to the Canadian Guild of Crafts and then, on expeditions he made to camps and settlements, first for the Guild and then as a Canadian government officer, he asked for carvings to sell in the south. He first visited Cape Dorset in 1951 and, perhaps impressed by the talent of the people, from 1957 until 1962 when he left the Arctic, made his headquarters there. In 1957, he and a small group of Dorset artists began their exciting experiments in print-making.

ᑐᖕᒪᕐᖕᐃᖅ). ᐱᕐᐅᑕᖅ ᐅᑲᑐᒥᕐᕜ ᐊᒪᕐᕐᐊᕐᑦ ᑎᑎᑐᖕᐊ ᖅᐸᓂ; ᐊᒡᓗᑎᖅ ᐅᖅᐅᕐᖅᑲᑐᒥᕐ ᐱᐅᕐᖃᓪᕐᒡᐊ ᒪᖅᓂ ᖃᓂᐊᓂ: ᐱᐳᓐᕐᖅ ᐅᖅᖃᓚᑎᓂᑲᐅᑐᕐᖅ ᖃᐊᒥᕐ ᕆᕐᖄᓂ, ᒪ ᐃᖃᓇᐊᕐᖃᑐ ᐊᓚᐱᓂᕐᓂ, ᓂᐅᑐᕐᖅᒥᕐ ᐊᕐᐊᑎᖃ ᓇᓇᓂ, ᐊᕐᒍᐊᑦ 1950 ᐱᕐᐊᓗᑎᓐᖕᓂᕐᑦ ᕆᕐᐳᑭᐅᕐ ᐃᓇᑎᕐᖃᕐ ᐃᓄᐊᑦ ᓇᓇᓂ ᓇᓇᕐᖁᕐ ᐊᒡᓗ ᑎᑎ ᐅᖃᐅᕐᕜ ᖃᐊᒐᐊᓂ ᐊᓗᕐᖅ ᐃᓄᐊᑦ ᓇᓇᑕ ᑯᐳᐊᖅᓂ.

ᑕᑯᐊ ᑕᒪᕐᖅ ᐱᒍᕐᕐᒪᕐ ᐱᕆᐊᖃᓂᕐ ᐱᒍᕐᖕᐁᖕᖅ ᖅᒪᐃᕐ ᐅᖃᖅᑐᐊᓂᖅ. ᖃᐊᒥᕐ ᕆᕐᖄᕐ ᖃᓇ ᕐᖕᐅᕐᕐᒦ ᐱᒍᕐᖕᐁᖅᒪᖅ ᐊᑐᓕᕐᖅᓈᕐᖓ ᓇᑎᓂᕐ ᑭᓇ ᓇᓇ. ᑕᑯᐊ 100-ᓂᕐ ᐊᕐᒍᓂᕐ ᐱᑐᖕᐁᕐᒥᕐᖅᑐ ᐃᖃᓇᐊᕐᕐᐁ ᐅᑐᓄᖃ ᖅᐊᒨᓂᕐ ᐊᒡᓗ ᐊᕐᒍᕐᒃ 19-ᓂᕐ ᓂᐅᑐᖕᑲᕐᕐᓕᓄᑐ ᐊᕐᕐᓂᕐ ᕆᕐᖄᕐᕐ ᑐᑐᓂᕐ ᓇᐸᓂᕐ, ᐃᓄᓇᕐᕐ ᓇᑕᐅᕆᕐᕐᓂᕐ ᑎᑎᑐᓂᕐ, ᓂᐅᑐᖕᑲᕐᒥᕐᖅ ᐅᕐᒪᕐᐊᖅᐊᕐᕐᐅᖓᕐᕐᑦ. ᕐᖕᐅᕐᕐᐁ ᕆᕐᖄᕐᕐᒥ ᑲᑐᖕᐅᐱᕐᖄᕐᕐᖅ ᐃᓄᐊᑦ ᓇᐸᓂᕐ 1940 ᐊᕐᒍᐊ ᐱᕆᐊᕐᖁᕐᕐᐸᑐᑐᕐᕐᓂᕐ ᑎᑎᑐᖕᐊᖅᐸᕐᕐᓕᕐᕜᒻ ᐃᓄᐊᑦ ᓇᓇᓂᕐ. ᐅᑎᑎᒥᕐᕜᕐᑐᐅᕐᑐ ᑕᐃᓚᐊᖓᓂᕐᖅ ᖃᓇᑐᕆᐱᐊᓂᕐ ᓇᑎᐊᓗᐊᑭᐊᑐᕐᖁᕐᓂᕐ ᐊᒡᓗ ᑕᐃᓚᐊ ᐊᕐᐅᑐᕐᖕᐁᐊ ᐃᓄᐊᑦ ᓇᓇᕐᖕᐊ ᐊᒡᓗ ᐃᑐᓄ ᑐᕐᕐᕐᐅᖅᕐᕜᒃ, ᕆᕐᐳᑭᐊᕆᒻ ᐃᑲᕐᑐᐅᕐᕐᒃ ᐊᒡᓗ ᑕᐃᓚᐊ ᖃᓇᑐᕆᐱᐊᓂᕐ ᑭᕐᓇᕐᐁᒻ ᐃᓄᐁᑎᒥᕐᕜᕐᑐᕐᖕᐁ, ᑕᓇ ᐊᕐᖕᐁᑎᑐᐅᕐᑦ

Going after fish (detail).
Felt pen, 1970

ᐃᖃᓗᒐᐅᑦ (ᐃᒪᐃᓕᒍᓕᒪ)
ᐊᒪᕈᔾ ᐊᓴᐅᑎᔾ ᑎᑎᑐᒪ, 1970

Terrence Ryan came later to Cape Dorset. He arrived in 1960 as a summer art student and remained when the Eskimos asked him to stay. Under his stewardship the Co-operative has strengthened and demand and interest in the Dorset graphics have greatly increased. As a result, the Co-operative helps sustain the community as Eskimos move from a hunting culture to the computer age. Like Pitseolak, many of the artists feel great loyalty to their 'Co-op'. (The Co-operative's headquarters, a small building in the centre of the community with a dazzling white, yellow and blue optical colour scheme, is always crowded with carvers and print-makers bringing in their work and, like artists everywhere, looking quite critically at the work of others!) As art director, Ryan, who doubles as the area's justice of the peace, has made it his policy to restrict his influence and, in assessing the accomplishment of the print-making years, he says, "Perhaps for the long term the great achievement has been in saving a record of what the Dorset people have been able to say graphically at this time."

ᓴᐅᑎᑲᒪᒪ ᓂᐅᑐᑎᓴᖅ ᑲᓄᑦ ᓄᓇᒐ. ᑲᓇ ᕆᐅᒐᕙᒥ ᓂᐅᑐᕆᐊᓗᑎᑎᐅᕐᒐ ᑭᓗᓂᑦ 1951-ᒍᑐᒍ ᐊᒪᓗ, ᐃᒪᑲ ᐱᓇᕐᑕᕆᕐᕙᓂ ᑲᐅᕆᓗᕆᓇ ᐃᓄᐃ, ᐱᕿᕗᑎᓐᑯ 1957-ᒥ ᓄᑲᕐᑎ 1962-ᒥ ᐊᐅᓕᒪ ᓴᕆᒥ ᑭᓚᐃᕙᓂ ᐃᓄᐃ ᓄᓇᓗᓂ, ᑕᐃᑲᓂᓚᓂ 1957-ᒥ ᕙᕐᑕ ᐊᒪᓗ ᐃᑭᓗᓐᑲ ᑭᓗᒥᐅᑦ ᓴᓇᒍᐊᑎᑦ ᐱᓯᐊᕐᑲᐅᑦᑎᑦ ᑲᐅᕐᓴᕐᑎ ᑎᑎᑐᕐᑲᑎᓂᒥ.

ᑎᑎᑕ ᐅᑦᐊᕐᕙᓇ ᑎᕆᓯᕐᑎᕐᕙᑦ ᕆᐊᕆ ᑭᓗᒪ. ᑎᕆᓯᕐᕙᑐ 1960-ᑐᑐᒍ ᐊᐅᕐᕿᑦ ᑎᑎᑐᕐᓴᒥ ᐃᓴᓂᐊᕐᓯ ᐊᒪᓗ ᑕᐃᑯᓂᐊᕐᕿᑐ ᐃᓄᕙᑦ ᐊᐱᓇᓴᕐᑎᒥ ᑕᐃᑯᓂᑲᕐᑐᐊᓇ ᑲᓂᒥ. ᑯᐊᕝᑲᓇᕐᑕᓚᑦ ᑯᑐᐊᕿ ᕆᒐᕐᑐᑐᕐ ᐊᒪᓗ ᐱᒍᕐᑕᕿᑐᑎ ᐃᐅᕐᕿᑐᑐᓄ ᑭᓗᒥᓴ ᑎᑎᑐᕐᕙ ᐊᕆᕿᑯᒥ ᐊᕆᓇᑎ. ᐊᕿᓄᕆᒐᓗ ᑲᓇ ᑯᐅᕿᕐ ᐊᑲᕿᕐᑕᑐ ᐱᒍᑕᑕᕐᓂ ᓄᐊᓚᓂ ᐃᓄᐊᑦ ᕿᕐᓚᕆᓚᑦ ᐊᒐᓇᕿᓇᕐᑦ ᐊᕙᕿᓚᐅ ᐊᑯᑕᓇ ᓴᒍᕐᑎᖅ. ᐃᓇᐅ ᐊᕆᕙᕿᑎᑦ ᐊᕐᕆ ᑎᑎᑐᕐᓇᑦ ᐊᕆᓂᓚᑦ ᐊᕿᕆᕙᑐ ᐃᑲᕐᕆᕐᕙᐅᕆᐊᕐᕆᓄ ᑯᑐᐊᕝᒥᓂ. (ᑲᓇ ᑯᑐᐊᕿᐊᑦ ᐊᓕᕿᑭᐊᓇᓚ, ᒦᕿᑐᔪ ᐃᕐᓴ ᓄᐊᑦ ᕿᑎᓂᓚᑦ ᕿᑕᑕᕆᓂᒥ ᒍᒐᕿᓚᕿ ᕿᕆᑎᒥ ᑐᒍᐊᕿᓚ ᑕᑯᕆᑐᐊᕿᑦ ᑕᐅᓚ ᒍᒐᕿᓚᕿ ᑕᐊᓚᑎᕐᓚ ᓄᓂᐅᑐᕝ ᓴᒍᐊᕿ ᑎᑎᑐᕐᓴᓄ ᑕᐊᑯᓚᐊᕆᓂ ᐱᓇᕐᕿᑕᕐᓂᒥ ᕿᕆᕆᐊᕿᓄᓗ, ᑕᐊᓚᓴᐊᕿ ᓴᒍᐊᕿᓇ ᑕᐊᓚᐊᕿ

Bringing home the catch.
Coloured pencil and felt pen,
ca. 1967

ᓂᕆᖕᒃ ᐊᓂᖅᑐᐃᖅᒃ
ᑕᖅᓴᓪᓗ ᐊᓪᓗ ᐃᓪᓕᒍᒃ ᐊᓕᑎᓄᒃ
ᑎᑎᒐᒻ, I967 ᑐᓐᒍ

The first Dorset graphics were offered for sale in 1958 at Ontario's Stratford Festival; each year since has seen an edition of stone cuts, stencils and, after 1962, copper engravings. The Eskimos' radically new style of life means that for the first time they need paychecks and Pitseolak makes no bones about what the prints have meant to her: they have brought her money. But just as emphatically she says they have made her happy. In these difficult times they have provided the sense of pride that goes with work well done.

Readers may notice that in her story Pitseolak never uses dates. Like most Eskimos of her generation, she relates all events to other important happenings – the building of the first Hudson's Bay Company buildings (1913); the sinking of the Hudson's Bay supply ship, the 'Nascopie' (1947); the completion of what in Cape Dorset is known as Pootagook's church (1953). Thus, the white people began to appear in great numbers in the North in the fifties – after the Nascopie went down.

ᐊᕆᑐᐃᐊ, ᐊᐃᑎᔅᑲᓱᒃᑐᕐᑎᖕᒃ ᐃᖃᐊᐅᖅ(ᖁᖅ ᐊᕐᕿᓂ!) ᐊᓪᕿᑲᔪᕐᓄ ᓴᐊᔪᐊᓄ ᐅᕿᐊᕐᖃ ᐃᓗᐊᑐᕐᑭ ᐊᓄᐅᖅᓱᑐᖅ, ᐊᓪᓗ ᐊᕿᕿᓂ ᐊᕿᕿᖕᒃ ᑕᑯᐊ ᐱᕿᐊᕐᕿᖕᒃ ᑕᐃᒪᓇᐊᖅ ᑎᑎᑐᐅᐊᖕᒃ ᓴᕿᐊᓂᕿᖕᒃ ᐊᖅᒍᓂ, ᐅᖃᓱᓂ ᑕᓇ, "ᐃᓪᖕᒃ ᐊᖕᓇᐊᓱᖕᒃ ᐃᖕᐅᓇᐅᑦᖕᓴᓐᓄ ᐅᖕᖅᑐᐅᕐᓚᕿᖕᒃ ᐃᖕᐅᓚᔪᓂᕿᓄᕿ ᖃᓄ ᕿᓕᕐᑐᕿ ᐃᓄᐃᕿ ᐅᖕᑲᓇᓂᓪᓕᕿ ᓴᐊᐅᓗ ᓚᐊᐅᖅᑐ".

ᑕᑯᐊ ᕿᐅᕿᐊᕐᒻ ᕿᓕᓂ ᓴᐊᐅᓚᐃ ᓂᐅᐅᑎᓂᕐᐅᖅᐊᖅ I958-ᔪᓂᐅᔪ ᐊᖕᑎᐅᑎᐅᒻ ᓄᐊᒻ ᐊᖅᒍᑕᓪ ᑕᐃᖕᓄ ᑕᕿᖅᐅᕐᓚ ᖁᐅ ᐊᕿᕿᓚᓂᒻ ᐅᕐᖅᐊᕿ ᖃᖕᕿᓚᕿ ᑕᕐᐅᐊᔪᓄᐅᓪ, I962-ᔪᕐᕿᓗᐅᑐᔪ ᖃᕿᓐᕿᕿ ᐊᕐᕿᐅᕐᐅᑎᕿᕐᒍᔾ. ᐊᕿᐅᐃ ᕿᐊᐅᐊ ᑎᕿᓪᐊᕐᖅᓇᐅᔪ ᑕᑯᐊ ᑎᑎᑐᕿᐊ ᕐᕿᖕᐅ; ᕿᐊᐅᕐᖅᑕᓐᑕᐅᐊᐅᔪ. ᐊᓚ ᓂᐊᔭ ᐃᐊᕐᓗᕿ ᐅᖕᐅᓇ ᐐᐊᐊᕐᑎᓐᑕᐅᓇᖕᓪᕐᕿ. ᐊᖕᐅᔪᐊᐊᑎ ᓪᔪ ᐃᖕᕿᕿᖕ ᑖᓪᑲ ᐊᕿᐅᓚᐅᔪ ᐊᕿᐊᐃᕿᓚᒍᓪ ᐐᕐᐊᕐᓚᐅᓂ.

ᐅᖃᓚᑎᓪ ᖃᐊᕿᓚᕿᓇᐅᔭᐃᓪ ᐅᐊᖅᑐᐊᓚᓇᖕᒃ ᐱᕿᐅᖕᒃ, ᑕᐱᒻ ᐊᔪᖃᕿᓚᕿᒻᒻᓚ ᐅᖕᓗᓇᒻ. ᑕᑯᐊᖕᑐ ᐃᓚᓇᖕᕿᖕᒃ ᐃᖕᐃᕿ ᕿᔪᖕᐃᕿᒻᒻ, ᐱᕿᐅᖕᒃ ᐃᓚᑐᕿᕐᕿᖕᒃ ᐃᖕᓇᕿᓂ ᐊᔾᕿᐅᐊᖕᐅᐅᖕᒃ ᐊᕿᕿᓂ ᐱᕿᔪᐊᔪᒻ ᐊᔾᕿᐅᐊᖕᐅᐅᖕᓇ -- ᑕᐊᐊ ᐊᖕᒃ ᓂᐅᕿᐊᕐᒻ

Three translators worked on Pitseolak's story. After the first day, Quatsia retired, explaining that she didn't know the Eskimo words for the old things and the old ways. Another young Eskimo woman, Annie Manning, took her place. Annie didn't know all the old words either, but she liked the work. "It's interesting," she remarked, "finding out about the old way." Finally, in order to preserve flavour and nuance as completely as possible, the taped interviews were re-translated word for word by Ann Hanson, justly famous in the Northwest Territories as an interpreter. Related to many of the Cape Dorset people, Ann was born in Lake Harbour and, after her parents died, went to school in Toronto. She translated for the Royal Family during their 1970 visit to Frobisher Bay.

As preparations for the publication of Pitseolak's story proceeded, it was decided that the book should appear in an Eskimo/English edition. The Eskimo text was prepared by Sarah Ekoomiak and Harriet Ruston of the Department of Indian Affairs and Northern Development.

ᓂᐅᐱᐅᑎᑯ ᐊᑕ ᔱᑲᐊᓂᓂ I9I3-ᒍᑎᔪ ᑭᐱᔝᐊᓂᑫ
ᓂᐅᐱᐅᑎᑯ ᐅᒥᐊᕈᐊᓪᓂᑲ ᓂᐅᐱᐊᕙᓂ ᐅᕐᓂ, ᓀᕈᐱᐊᒥ,
I947-ᒍᑎᔪ ᐱᔝᑎᒍᑲᕐᓂ ᑲᐅᐊᑐᓂᓪᓂᑲ ᑭᓂ ᑲᐅᕕᒪ
ᔝᐅᕁ ᔪᑐᔫ ᔪᕿᐊᒪ I953. ᑕᐱᒪᓇᑕ ᑲᔱᓂᑦ
ᐊᒡᕈᐨᕙᓐᐊᕈᓂᑕ ᐃᓄᐊᑦ ᓀᓂᓂ I950-ᐅᓀᑎᒋ ᐊᕿᒍᐊ
-- ᐊᒪᔪ ᓀᕈᑎᐱ ᑭᐊᕈᓇᑎᔪ.

ᐱᒥᕈ ᔪᕁᐊᑦ ᐱᓂᕈᐊᓇᐅᔪ ᐱᕈᐅᓀᑦ ᐅᓂᑲᔪᐊᓂᓇ. ᐅᑲ ᔪᕁᐊᔪᑕᐊᑦ ᒋᔪᓂᓂᓂ, ᑯᐊᕈᐊ ᓂᑲᓀᐅᔪ ᐅᑲᓪᓇ ᑲᐅᕙᒪᓂᒪᔪ ᐃᓄᐊᑦ ᐅᓂᑲᐅᕈᓂᑲ ᐅᕙᕈᐊᔪᓇᑕ ᐊᒪᔪ ᐃᓂᕈᐊᕁᑫ. ᐊᕈᒪᑕᕁ ᐃᓂᕈ ᐃᓂᑲ ᐊᕁᓇ, ᐊᓂ ᓪᓂᕁ ᐃᓂᕈᕈᐊᐅᔪᕁ ᔪᐊᕈᐊᒥ. ᐊᓂ ᑲᐅᕙᒪᓪᓀᐅᕐᕈᔝᐊᑐ ᐃᓇᓂᓂ ᐅᑲᐅᕈᔪᓇ ᐃᐊ ᐱᐅᕈᓀᐊᑐ ᐃᓇᓀᐅᕁᓂᓂᓇᕁ. "ᔪᕁᒍᕙᓇᕙᓪᔪᐊᑦ" ᐊᓂ ᓇᓀᐅᑐᕁ "ᑲᐅᕙᒪᒪᕈᐊᑲᕁᓇᔪ ᐃᓂᕈᔪᕁᐅᕁ ᕁᓀᓂᑦ" ᐱᕈᕁ ᕁᔝᓂᐊᓇᑐᕁ, ᐊᕈᕈᓀᒪ ᐊᒪᔪ ᔪᑭᕙᒪᕈᕙᑐᔪ ᐊᕙᓂᕈ ᐊᔝᐊᑦ, ᑕᕈᔪᒪ ᓂᐱᓂᐅᕈᕁᒪᔪᐨ ᐊᐅᕁᕈᓀᐊᐅᓂᓂᑕ ᑲᔪᓇᑐᓇᓪᓂᓀᐅᕁᓇᓀᐊᔪᐨ ᐅᕁᕁᒋᕈ ᐊᕈ ᐊᓇᔪᓪ ᐃᓇᕈ ᓂ ᑲᐅᕙᒪᕁᔝᕈᐊᔪ ᐃᓄᐊᑦ ᓇᕈᓂᕁ ᓀᕙᕈᐊᒥ ᔪᕁᔝᐅᕈᐊᕁᕁ. ᐃᓂᑲᔪᒥ ᐊᒪᕁᓂ ᑭᓪᒪᐅᕈᒥ ᐃᓇᕈ, ᐊᕈ ᐃᓀᑲᐅᔪ ᑭᒪᕈᕁ ᐊᒪᔪ ᐊᑐᑐᕈᕁ ᔪᑯᓪᓀᓇᔪᕁ ᐃᓇᓀᐊᕈᐊᐅᔪ ᔪᔝᓇᒪᕁ.

Readers may be interested to know that syllabics, the phonetic system of writing used by the Eskimos, was introduced by the missionaries in the late nineteenth century. Long before schools came to the Eastern Arctic, nine out of ten Eskimos could read and write in their own language.

Perhaps, in fact probably, not all the people mentioned in Pitseolak's account of her extraordinary life will remember events exactly as she does. But, hopefully, many books will come out of Cape Dorset. This is Pitseolak's story.

Dorothy Harley Eber
Montreal 1971

ᑕᓇᑕᒐ ᑐᓴᕈᕆᔭᐅᓚᐅᑐᒃ ᐊᑕᓂᐊᓗᑯᑦ ᑯᐃᓐ ᑭᑐᒐᕆᑦ ᓂᐅ ᕉᓯᒪᑎᓗᕆᑦ ᐃᑲᓗᓄᑦ 1970-ᒥ.

ᐊᑐᐃᓇᕈᑎᑕᐅᓂᒐ ᓄᓇᓕᓄ ᐊᑐᐊᒐᓴᓕᐊᒍᓂᐊᑎᓗᕆ ᐱᓯᐅᓚᑉ ᐅᓂᑲᑐᐊᓕᐊᑎᓯᔭᒐ, ᐅᑲᑕᐅᓯᓚᐅᑐ ᑕᓇ ᐅᓂᑲᑐᐊ ᐃᓄᑎᑐᓕ ᒐᕙᓴᐅᑯᓯᒍ ᑲᓗᓇᑎᑐᑦ ᐊᑭᓯᒪᓂᒐ. ᑕᓯᒪ ᐃᓄᒃᑎᑐᓂᒐ ᑎᑎᕋᓯᒪᓂᒐ ᐊᑭᑕᐅᓚᐅᑐᒃ ᓯᐊᔭ ᐃᕈᒥᐊᒃ ᑲᕈᐊ ᐅᕋᓴ ᑕᓐ ᒧᓗ ᐃᓄᓕᑎᕈᑯᓂᒥᐅᓄᑦ.

ᐃᒪᒃ ᐃᓗᓇᕆᓂᐅᕙᓴᐅᕆᑐᒃ ᐃᓄᓂ ᐅᑲᓯᒪᕙᒃ ᐱᓯᐅᓚᑉ ᐅᑲᐅᓯᑎᔭᒐ ᐃᓄᓯᑎᓯᒪᔭᒥᓂ ᐊᐅᓚᕈᓇᓚᒐᕗ ᑲᓄᓯᐊᒃ ᐱᒍᓯ ᕆᔭᒥᓂ. ᐃᓚ ᐊᒥᓯᑯᒥᓇᑐᒐᓗᐊ, ᐅᑲᓕᒪᒐᐃ ᑭᒐᓂ ᐱᓚᑐᐃ. ᑕᓇ ᑕᕙ ᐱᓯᐅᓚᑉ ᐅᓂᑲᑐᐊᒐ.

ᑕᓯ ᕋᐃᓕ ᐃᒃᐳ
ᐊᑭᓯᐃᕈᒃ

Birds of summer.
Engraving, 1964

ᐊᐅᔭᒥ ᑯᐸᓄᐊᑦ
ᐅᑯᓯᓴᔭᒥ ᑎᑎᑐᒐ, I964

My name is Pitseolak, the Eskimo word for the sea pigeon. When I see pitseolaks over the sea, I say, "There go those lovely birds – that's me, flying!"

I have lost the time when I was born but I am old now – my sons say maybe I am 70. When Ashoona, my husband, died, my sons were not even married. Now they are married and having their children.

I became an artist to earn money but I think I am a real artist. Even when they are out of papers for drawing at the Co-op, they find papers for me. I draw the things I have never seen, the monsters and spirits, and I draw the old ways, the things we did long ago before there were many white men. I don't know how many drawings I have done but more than a thousand. There are many Pitseolaks now – I have signed my name many times.

I was born on Nottingham Island in Hudson's Bay. The year I was born my parents and three brothers began a long

ᐱᓯᐅᓚᒍᕗᒐ ᐊᒪᓗ ᑕᑯᒐᒪ ᐱᓯᐅᓚᓂ ᐃᒪᑯᑐᓂ, ᐅᑲᓗᒐ,
"ᐃᑯᐊᑕᒐ ᑯᐸᓄᐊᑯᓗᐃᑦ ᐅᕙᒐᐅᓇ, ᑎᒥᕙᒃ!"

ᐃᑲᐅᒪᒍᓇᒋᑐᒐ ᐃᓚᒐᓂ ᐃᓄᓕᓚᐅᕋᒪ ᐃᓚ ᒪᓇ ᓂᒋᐅᒍᓕᑐᒐ ᐃᒃᓂᒐ ᐅᑲᒪ ᐃᒪᑲ 70-ᓂ ᐅᑭᐅᑲᑐᒐ. ᐊᒃᓱᓇ ᐅᐃᒐ, ᑐᑯᑎᓗᒍ ᐃᒃᓂᑲ ᓄᓕᐊᑲᓚᐅᒋᑐᐃᓗᓂ. ᒪᓇᓕ ᓄᓕᐊᑲᓕᐳᑦ ᐱᐊᕋᑲᓕᓗᑎᓗ.

ᑭᓇᐅᔭᓚᐅᕋᓯᓗᒐ ᑭᓯᐊᓂ ᑎᑎᑐᔭᑎᒍᓚᐅᑐᒐ ᐃᓚ ᐃᓱᒪᕙᒐ ᑎᑎᑐᔭᑎᓗᑐᒋᐊᓴ. ᐸᐃᐸᓂ ᓄᒍᒍᔭᐅᒐᓗᐊᒪᑕ ᑎᑎᑐᔭᕕᓴᓂ ᑯᐅᐊᐸᒥ, ᐅᕙᓄ ᓇᓂᓯᒍᔭᐅᕙᐳᒐ ᑎᑎᑐᔭᐸᑲᒪ ᑭᓯᑐᐃᓇᓂ ᑕᑯᓚᐅᓯᒪᒋᒪᑎᑕᓂ, ᑐᒐᓂ ᐊᒐᑯᓂᓗ, ᐊᒪᓗ ᑎᑎᑐᔭᓗᒐ ᐱᐅᓯᐅᕙᑐᕕᓂᓂᒃ, ᑭᓯᑐᐃᓇᓂᒃ ᐊᑐᐸᓚᐅᑕᑎᓂᒃ ᐅᕙᓯᐊᕈ ᐊᒥᓯᓂᒃ ᑲᓗᓇᑲᓚᐅᑎᓇᒍ. ᑲᐅᐅᒪᒋᑐᒐ ᑲᓯᓂ ᑎᑎᑐᔭᓯᒪᓕ ᒪᒐᒪ ᐃᓚ I000 ᐅᓄᓂᓴᓂ. ᒪᓇᓕ ᐊᒥᓱᓂ ᐱᓯᐅᓚᑲᓕᑐ ᑎᑎᓯᓯᒪᒐᒪ ᐊᑎᖁᓂ ᐊᒥᓱᕕᓱᒐ.

ᐃᓄᓕᓚᐅᓯᒪᕗᒐ ᑐᔭᓂ ᐃᓄᐃᑦ ᓄᓇᒐᑕ ᑕᖁᓂ. ᑕᓇ ᐊᖁᒍᑎᓗᒍ ᐃᓄᓕᕕᒋᓚᐅᑕᒐ ᐊᑕᑕᑯᑲ ᐊᒪᓗ ᐱᒐᓱᑦ ᐊᓂᑲ ᐊᐅᓚᑎᐊᓯᓚᐅᓯᒪᕙ ᐅᒐᓯᑐᐊᓗᒍ. ᑭᒪᐃᓱᑎ ᓄᓇᒥᓂ ᓴᒃ ᓗᓂ

trip. They left their camp in Sugluk on the coast of Quebec
and set out for Baffin Island to join relatives. They left
in the spring and reached Nottingham Island where I was
born. The next spring they crossed the Hudson Strait
and arrived in the Foxe Peninsula, in the place where Cape
Dorset is today.

But our journey was not quite ended for, the next spring,
we continued along the Hudson Strait and reached
Frobisher Bay. That was when there were no white men
there at all.

These were long journeys and dangerous, too, when the
waters were rough, but I didn't know – I was still being
carried on the back of my mother.

We made all these travels in a sealskin boat. Such boats
had wooden frames that were covered with skins. They
used to be called the women's boats because they were
sewn by the women. Many women sewed to make one

ᑯᐸᐃᒃ ᑐᑭᐊᓂ ᐊᒡᓗ ᓄᓇᑐᓂ ᐃᓄᐃ ᓄᓇᕐᕿᒥ ᓄᓇᕐᐊᒥ
ᑲᑎᕐᓱᓂ ᐃᓕᒐᓂ. ᐊᐅᑦᑕᐅᑐ ᐅᐱᒪᓱᓕᒥ ᐊᐅᑐᓂᒥᓇᒃ
ᐃᓄᐃᑦ ᓄᓇᒪᑕ ᑭᑕᒍ ᐊᒡᓗ ᑎᑭᓴᑎ ᐳᐊᕐ ᐱᓂᕐᓚᒍ ᑕᓇ
ᓄᓇ ᑕᕙᓂ ᑭᒪᐅᑐᒃ ᒪᓇ.

ᐃᓚ ᐊᐅᑯᓂᑕᐅᑕᐅᑦ ᓇᕐᐊᑕᐅᒥᕐᕸᒃ ᐅᐱᒍᓇᐊᓯᕐᕸᒍ,
ᐊᐅᓚᕿᐊᓱᑦ ᐃᓄᐃ ᓄᓇᒪᑕ ᑭᑕᒍ ᐊᒡᓗ ᑎᑭᓱᑕ ᐊᕿᓱᓄᑦ.
ᑕᐊᕐᒪᓂ ᑲᓱᐊᕿᑲᐅᕐᓚᕐᕐᐊᑕᕿ.

ᑕᑯᐊ ᐅᒪᕐᕼᒍᓚ ᐊᐅᑯᓂᑕᐅᑕᐅᑦ ᑲᐱᕋᐊᑐᐊᓱᓂᕐᕼᕿ ᐊᓚᐃᑦ
ᐊᕐᕐᐊᑐᐊᓱᓂᓱᕐ ᐃᓚ ᑲᐳᕐᓚᕐᑐᓚ – – ᕸᓚ ᐊᓚᑕᐅᑕᐅᕼᒪᓚ
ᐊᓇᓇᕐᕿ.

ᑕᑯᐊᕼᒥᓚ ᐊᐅᑯᓂᑕᐅᑕᐅᑦ ᓇᕐᐅᕸ ᕿᕐᓚᒥ ᐅᒥᐊᕿᕐᑕ.
ᑕᐊᒪᐊᑐᕸ ᐅᒥᐊᕿ ᕿᕐᒥ ᐊᑕᒍᑎᕿᓂᓱᒍ ᕿᕐᒥ ᐊᕐᒥᐊᕿᓄᓇᕿ.
ᑕᐃᕐᐅᕹᕼᑕᐅᑐᕿ ᐊᕿᓇᐊᐃᑦ ᐅᒥᐊᒡᓚ ᒥᓕᑕᐅᕼᒪᓚᓚᕿ ᐊᕿᓇᐊᕐᕿ.
ᐊᕿᕿ ᐊᕿᓇᐊᐃᑦ ᒥᓱᕼᕸᑕᐅᑐ ᐊᑕᐅᕼᒥ ᐅᒥᐊᑕᐅᑐᕼᑎ. ᐅᒥᐊᕿ

Mother with child.
Felt pen, 1970

Crossing the Straits.
Stone cut, 1970

ᐊᑲᖅ ᐱᒥᓴᐅᑲᕝᔭᓚᐅᒍ ᑭᒐᐅᓚᐅ ᐊᑭᐊᐱᔪᓗᓂ ᑭᕐᐊᓐ
ᐱᒥᓴᐅᑲᕝᔭᓚᐅᕋᓐ ᐊᐅᓚᐅᑎᒃᓚᓚ ᑕᐊᓪ ᐊᑦᑕᓪ ᐊᓂᕐ
ᐸᒍᕝᔭᐅᒍᕝ ᑐᐳᓚᓚᔭᓗᕝ. ᕐᔭᐅ ᑐᕝᑲᑦᕝᓯ ᐅᑲᓐᔪᕐ
ᐅᒐᐊᕝ ᐊᕝᔭᐊᓯᕝ ᑕᑕᕝᐊᒍᕝᑦ!

ᐊᑕ ᐱᐊᕐᐅᑎᓗᓚᓯ ᑕᔾᐊ ᓪᕐᐅᕝ ᑭᓭᕝ ᐅᒐᐊᕝ ᐱᑕᕝᕝ
ᔪᓗᑲᐅᑐ. ᕐᔭᑦᑲᕝ ᐊᐅᑲᕝᐳᒐ ᐊᓪᕐᓭᓂ ᐊᒐ ᓂᕝᕝᕐ
ᑭᒐᒐ ᐊᕝᒐᓚᕐᕝᑦ ᑭᒐᓂ ᓂᐅᐱᓐᕝᕐᕝ ᑭᕝᕐ ᐅᒐᐊᕝ.
ᑕᐊᕝᓂ ᐊᕐᕐᕝᑲᕝᔭᐅᒍᕝ. ᐊᑦᑕᓪ ᐅᒐᐊᒐᓭᑎᓚᒍ ᑭᕝᕝ,
ᐅᒐᐊᒐ ᑕᑦᕐᐊᒐᐅᕐᕝᓚᕝᓪ ᐊᓪᓚ ᐊᕝᓭᓂ ᑕᑦᕐᐊᒐᐅᕐᕝᓚᕝᓪ
ᕝᓭᓚᕝᕝ ᑕᑦᕐᐅᕐᓯᒐ ᕝᐸᐊᕐᕐᐅᕐᕝᓚᕝᓪ.

ᐱᐊᕐᐳᕐᓪ ᐅᒐᐊᐳᕐᓚᓐᔪᓭᕝᐳᓪ ᓪᕐᐅᕝ ᑭᕝᓚᓂ ᐅᒐᐊ
ᐊᑕ ᑕᔾᐊ ᐊᑕᕝᑕᕝᕝ ᓐᓐᕝᕐᐸᕝᓯᓪ. ᐊᓪᕝ ᑕᔾᐊ ᐅᒐᐊᕝ
ᐊᕝᕐᐊᒐᓯᕝᕐᕐᑐᓗᔪᐊᕝ ᐊᕝᕐᐊᒐᓐᕐᕐᐊᓯᕝ ᐱᐊᕐᐅᕝᕝᕐᓚᕝᒍᕝ,
ᐊᕝᕐᐊᒐᕝᕝᕐᐊᐅᕝᓪᕝ ᑕᐊᓪᕝ ᐊᐅᑲᕝᕝᕝᑕᕝ. ᓐᓐᕝᕝᕝᕝᕝᐅᕝᓪ,
ᐅᕝᕝᐊᕝᓂᕝᑕᕝ ᑕᐊᓪᓚᓂᕝ ᕝᐅᕝᕝ -- ᕝᐊᕝᕝ ᕝᑎᕝᕝ --
ᓐᑎᕝᕝᐅᕝᓪᓪ ᐊᓪᓚ ᐊᕝᕝᐊᓯᐊ ᓐᓐᕝᕝᕝᕝᓚᕝᓪᕝ ᐅᕝᕝᒍᑕᕝᕝᓚᕝᓪ
ᐊᓪᓚ ᓐᓐᕝᕝᕝᕝᓚᓂᕝᓪᕝ. ᐊᓪᕝᓪ ᐊᓪᓂᕝᕝᕝ ᐊᕝᕝᓚᕝᓪ
ᐊᓪᕝᕝᕝᕝ ᕝᐅᕝ ᐊᓂᕝᑕᕝᕝ? ᐊᕝᓪᓂ! ᐊᕝᕝᐊᕝᕝ ᓚᕝᐊᕝᕝ:

boat. Some boats had sails made from the intestine of the
whale, but we had no sail and we had no motors then
so my father and brothers rowed all the way. Later, I often
heard them say the boat was very full!

But even in my childhood these sealskin boats were
already disappearing. My first memory of life is when we
stopped in Lake Harbour, on our way back from Frobisher
Bay to Cape Dorset, to buy a wooden boat. There were
many there. It was while my father bought the wooden
boat that I first saw houses and that I saw the first white
man. I was scared.

Only as a child was I ever in a sealskin boat, but I have
put these boats into my drawings. Perhaps these boats
were not really so big but to me, as a child, they seemed
very big and I remember them well. I have been drawing
the old ways since 'Sowmik' – Jim Houston – came,
and many of the drawings have been put on the stone
and turned into prints. Did I live all my remembered life in

Both in summer and winter we used to move a lot.
Felt pen, 1970

ᐊᐅᓯᒥ ᐅᑭᐅᒥᓗ ᓄᑲᑕᑎᓇᐸᓚᐅᔪᒍᑦ
ᐃᒪᓂᒧ ᐊᓚᐅᑎᒧᑦ ᑎᑎᑐᒐ, I970

the Foxe Peninsula? 'Ahalona!' . . . Very definitely! And most of my life I lived in the camps. I remember Cape Dorset when there weren't any houses. I remember when they were building the Hudson's Bay post. The same warehouses that are here now were built when my father and mother were still alive – when I was just a little girl.

Timungiak was my mother; Ottochie was my father. I had a happy childhood. I was always healthy and never sick. I had a large family – three brothers and a sister – and we were always happy to be together. We lived in the old Eskimo way. We would pick up and go to different camps – we were free to move anywhere and we lived in many camps. Sometimes they were near Cape Dorset and sometimes they were far away . . . it depended whether a person wanted to go far or to be near a settlement. My father hunted in the old way, too – with a bow and arrow. He had a shotgun but he didn't use it. Sometimes there were bad winters and we would go hungry but there was no starvation.

ᐊᒪᑕᐅᒃ ᐃᓄᓯᓂᓕᒪᑲᓴᒃ ᐃᓄᓯᒪᔭᒐ ᓄᓇᑎᓂ ᐃᒃ ᓗᑲᕆᑐᒥ ᑕᐃᑲᓂᓕᒪᒍᑲᑕᓚᐅᓯᒪᔭ ᓄᓇᒥ. ᐊᐅᓚᔮᔭᒐ ᑭᒐᐃᑦ ᐃᒃ ᓗᑕ ᑲᑎᓇᒍ. ᐊᐅᓚᔮᔭᒐ ᓂᐅᕕᑎᑯ ᐃᒃ ᓗᒐᓂ ᐃᒃ ᓗᓕᐅᑐᑲᑎᓗᒍ. ᑕᑯᐊᓴᐃᓇᐃᑦ ᑭᓯᑐᐃᓇᑲᐅᑎᐅᔭ ᒪᓇ ᐃᒃ ᓗᓕᐊᒍᓚᐅᓯᒪᔭ ᐊᑕᑕᒐ ᐊᓇᓇᒐᓗ ᓯᓕ ᐃᓄᑎᓗᕆ ᑕᒪᒥᒃ -- ᐱᑭᑐᑯᓗᓗᒐ ᓂᕕᐊᓯᐊᒍᑎᓗᒐ.

ᑎᒧᕆᐊᒃ ᐊᓇᓇᕆᓚᐅᓯᒪᔪᕋ; ᐅᒃᑐᑭ ᐊᑕᑕᕆᓚᐅᒃᓯᒪᔪᒐ. ᑯᕕᐊᓯᓚᐅᑐᒐ ᐱᐊᕋᐅᓯᒐ. ᑲᓄᐃᕆᓯᐊᕆᓇᓗᒐ ᑲᓂᒪᓚᐅᓯᒪᕆ ᓗᒐᓗ. ᐃᒪᓇ ᐅᓄᓂᑲᓚᐅᑐᒍ ᐃᓕᕆᓯᑕ ᐱᒐᓯᓂᒃ ᐊᓂᑲᓯᒐ ᐊᒪᓗ ᓄᑲᑲᓗᒐ -- ᐊᒪᓗ ᑕᐃᒪᒐᓕᒪᒃ ᑯᕕᐊᓯᐸᓚᐅᑐᒍᑦ ᑲᑎᒪᓯᑕ. ᐃᓄᓚᐅᑐᒍᑦ ᐃᓄᐃᑦ ᐃᓄᓯᑐᑲᒐᑎᑐ. ᐊᐅᓚᕆᓇᒃ ᑕᐸᓚᐅᑐᒍᑦ ᓇᒧᑐᐃᓇ ᐊᐃᕙᓯᑕ ᓄᓇᓄ--ᐃᓯᒪᐃᓇᑭᕙᓚᐅᑐᒍ ᓇᒧᑐᐃᓇᒃ ᓄᑲᑕᓯᑕ ᐊᒪᓗ ᓄᑲᐸᓯᑕ ᐊᔾᕆᕆᑐᓄᑦ ᓄᓇᓄ. ᐃᓚᓂ ᓄᓇᕗ ᑲᓂᑐᕙᓚᐅᑐ ᑭᒐᓄᑦ ᐊᒪᓗ ᐃᓚᓂ ᐅᒐᓯᑐᕙᓗᑕ ..ᓇᓕᐊᓄᑐᐃᓇ ᐃᓄᒃ ᐅᒐᓯᑐᒥᒍᒪᐸ ᐅᕙᓗᓂ ᑲᓂᑐᒥᒍᒪᐸ ᐃᒃ ᓗᑲᑐᒧᑦ. ᐊᑕᑕᒐ ᐊᒍᓇᓯᐊᐸᓚᐅᑐ ᐅᕙᓯᐊᕈᑎᑐᑕᐅ -- ᐱᑎᓯᒧ ᐱᑎᑕᒧᓗ. ᑯᑭᐅᑎᑲᓚᐅᓯᒪᔭ ᐃᓚ ᐊᑐᐸᓚᐅᕆᑕᒐ. ᐃᓚᓂᑯᑦ ᐅᑭᐅᒃ ᐱᐅᕙᓚᐅᕆᑐᑦ ᐃᓚᒐᓂᓗ ᑲᐸᓚᐅᓗᑕ ᐃᓚ ᐱᓕᑐᑲᓚᐅᓯᒪᕆᑐᒃ.

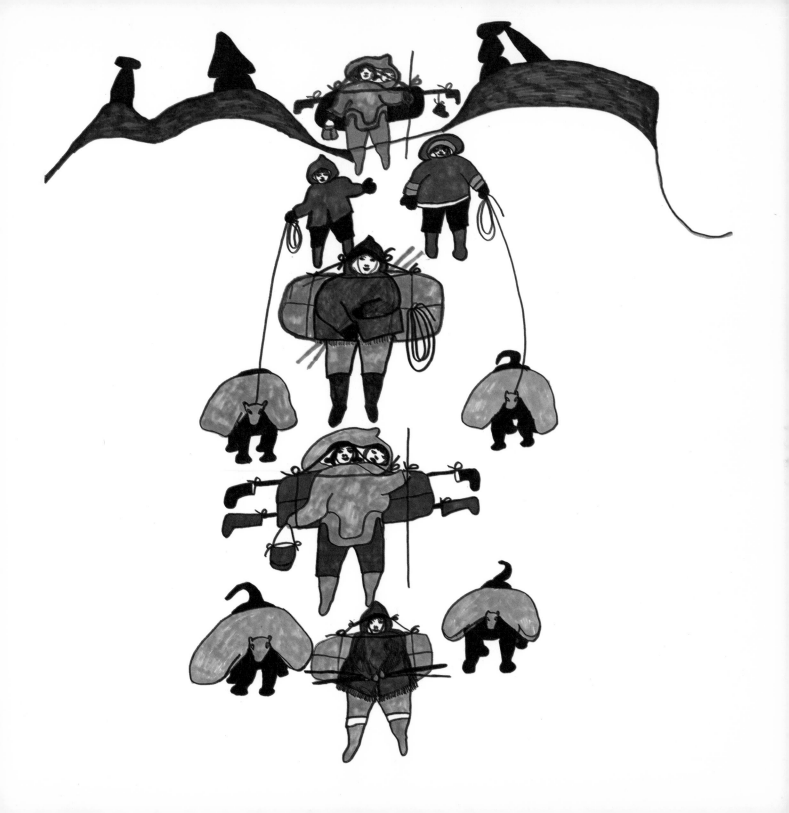

In those days many of the women had tattoo marks on
their faces and my mother had them, too. They used to do
it with a needle and caribou thread soaked in oil and soot
from the 'kudlik' – the seal oil lamp. They used to pull
the thread through the skin and the skin would be swollen
for many days. I don't know exactly why people had
tattoos but I believe the women did it because they thought
it was pretty. I did, too. When I was young I tried a few
marks on my arm, as you can see.

My father used to tell stories about how he was once
almost killed by a powerful shaman. My father was a very
good hunter and that is why the shaman tried to kill him –
he was jealous. I don't know very much about shamans
– I don't like to think about them – but my family and my
mother's family all believed in shamans because we had
heard so many stories. They were Eskimos just like other
people but they had these strange powers. They had
power over the hunt – they could bring the animals – and
they had power to kill. Just as it is today, a long time ago

From skins we made buckets
to carry water.
Coloured pencil and felt pen,
ca. 1967

ᑭᓯᐊᓂ ᐃᒪᑕᐅᑎᓱᖃᐅᐸᑕᐅᑐᒍᑦ
ᑲᖅᓴᓂᐅ ᐊᒥᓗ ᐃᒪᓕᒍ ᐊᑲᐅᑎᓄᐃᑦ
ᑎᑎᑐᒪ, 1967 ᐅᑎᓪᒍ

Bird attacking fish.
Coloured pencil and felt pen,
drawing for stone cut, 1969.

ᑯᐸᐊᑦ ᐃᖃᓗᐃᑦᑐᑦ
ᑲᖅᓴᓂᐅᑦ ᐊᒥᓗ ᐃᒪᓕᓄᑦ ᐊᑲᐅᑎᒍᑦ
ᑎᑎᑐᒪ ᑎᑎᑐᑉᑕᐅᑲᓐᓄ ᐅᑉᓴᒥ ᓴᓇᖅ
ᒪᐃᖅ 1969

Composition.
Engraving, 1964

ᐅᑯᕐᖅᖕᒥ ᓴᐅᖦᕐᐅᓂ, 1964

there was often hatred among people. When a shaman was jealous or hated another Eskimo, he would try to kill him and, sometimes, I think, if an Eskimo had an enemy in camp, he would go to a shaman friend and ask him to kill this man who hated him. But they were very good-looking people – you would really never believe they were shamans.

There were good shamans and bad shamans but most people feared them – in the old days there were many things to fear. Some people feared the animals, even the animals they ate. I always feared polar bears – they were scary.

When we were children we played lots of make-believe. We used to play igloo, we used to play dog-team. I think everybody plays these things. Perhaps children everywhere play the same things. We played a game in which other children would run after you; if they could catch you they would pretend to eat your eyes.

ᐃᓄᐃᑦ ᐃᓚᓐᖑᑦ. ᐊᒡᒃ ᐊᑦ ᐱᕐᖕᖕᑳᑯᑐᐊᒡᒥ ᐅᕕᔪᓂᑦ ᐅᒡᕐᓗᑦᑐᐊᒡᒥ ᐃᓄᑉᓂᖕᓂᒃ ᑐᑯᕐᓕᔭᐊᑕᑖᐱᓂ ᐊᒡᓗ ᐃᓚᓄᑦ ᐃᓄᑉ ᐅᒡᒥᖅᖃᑐᐊᒡᒥ ᓇᑲᓂᑐᒥ, ᐊᒡᒃᒍᑦ ᐊᐊᕃᑲᑐᑉ ᐱᑲᓐᒥᖕᖓ ᐅᖃᓗᓂ ᑐᑯᕐᒃᕐᒍ ᑕᕐᕕᒥ ᐊᒍᓐᒥ ᐅᒡᒥᖕᓕᖕᓂᒃ. ᐃᓚ ᑕᒡᐊ ᐃᓇᑕᓄᑉᕃᑲᑐᑉ ᐊᖕᕐᔪ ᐃᓄᐃ ᐅᐱᓇᖕᕋᑐᐊᓄ ᐊᒡᒃᒡᕐᐊᕐᓕᕐᑦ.

ᐱᐊᕐᓇᖕ ᐊᒡᒃᑉᐸᑕᑐᕐᒍᖕ ᐱᐊᕐᔪᐊᒍᓂ ᐊᒡᒃᑉᓂ ᐊᓕ ᐃᓄᓚᒡᒃᓄᖕᑦ ᐊᑉᕐᓕᖕᑐᐱᑲᑐᑉ -- ᐅᖕᕃᐊᕐ ᑕᐊᕐᖕᐅᑎᖕᒍ ᐊᒡᒥᖕᖕ ᑭᕐᑐᐊᖕᖕ ᐊᑉ ᕐᐊᓄᑉᕃᑲᑐᑉᑦ. ᐃᓚᕐᒃ ᐃᓄᐊ ᐊᑉᕃᑲᑐᑉ ᐅᒥᖕᖕᖕ ᓂᑦᕐᒥᖕᖕᐊᓕ ᐅᒥᖕᖕ ᐊᑉᕃᑲᑐᑉᑦ. ᑕᐊᓕᖕᑕᕐ ᐋᓇᖕ ᐊᑉᕃᕐᖕ. ᐋᓄᑐᖕᐊᑦ ᐊᑉ ᕐᐊᑲᑐᑉᕐᑦᑦ.

ᐱᐊᑕᖕᕐᑦ ᐱᒍᐊᑲᑐᑉᒍ ᐊᒡᒥᖕᖕ ᐅᐱᐊᒍᓂ. ᐱᒍᐊᑲᑐᑉᒍ ᐊᑉ ᖕᒡᐅᑐᒍᒍᐊᕐᑦᑦ, ᑮᒍᕐᒍᐊᕐᕐᑕᑦᒍ. ᐋᓄᓇᓕᑎ ᐃᓄᐊ ᑕᒡᒡᐊᖕᒡᒥ ᐱᒍᐊᕐᒍᑦᑐ. ᐊᒡᒥᖕ ᐱᐊᕐᓴᐊ ᓇᕐᑐᐊᐊ ᐱᒍᐊᕐᒍᒡ ᑕᒡᓄᖕᓕᐊᐊᖕ. ᐱᒍᐊᑲᑐᑉᒍ ᐱᒍᐊᖕᓐᖕᑦᕐᑦ ᐱᐊᑕᖕᖕᖕᓐᓐᖕ ᐅᖕᖕᑕᑕᓐᑦᕐᑦᑦ; ᐊᒍᖕᐊᒍᑦ ᐃᐊᑐᑕᒍᐊᓕᕐᑦᑦ.

From my father we used to learn the Eskimo legends.
There were many such stories and all children learn them,
but I have forgotten most of them now. I remember the
one about the blind boy who got back his eyesight when
a bird took him on his back and dived with him under
the sea three times. This blind young man lived with his
mother who was cruel to him and, when he returned home
and she saw he could see, this wicked mother was so
frightened she jumped into the sea. Eskimos believe she
became a white whale and is there still – they really
believe it.

There were no teenagers in those days. The young people
got married so early they didn't have time to make any
trouble. Now there are so many young boys and girls and
very often they are troublesome.

The year I married was the year my father died. He had
a bad sickness – it was something with the lower back –
and he died in our camp at Idjirituq. The year he died,

ᐊᑦᑕᒪᓄᑦ ᑲᐅᕐᓴᐸᑲᐅᐸᔪᑦ ᐃᓄᐊᑦ ᐅᓄᑲᑕᐅᒍᐲᒡᓂᐊᑦ.
ᐊᒡᓴᐊᓄᑉᐸᑲᐅᐸ ᑲᓄᐊᐲᐸᐃᓇᓂ ᐅᓄᑉᐊᓄ ᐊᓗ ᐱᐊᖂᓇᒪ
ᑲᐅᕐᓴᐸᑲᐅᑉᕐᑦ ᐃᓇ ᐳᐊᒍᒡᓚᓂᑲᑉ ᐃᓕᖁᑉᕐᑦ ᒪᓇ.
ᐊᐅᓯᐊᔨᒪ ᑕᐊᕐᒥᓚ ᕐᔪᕐᒥ ᑕᐅᒍᕐᒥᒡ ᑕᐅᒍᔪᓇᕐᐦᐊᓄᒥ
ᒍᓯᒍᒡᑉ ᒍᓄᐊᒍᑦ ᓄᑐᖃᐅᕐᓄ ᐊᓗᒡᑦ ᐱᓯᐸᐅᓄ ᐊᑉᑉᑕᐅ
ᑲᓄᖓᒥ ᑕᐅᒍᔪᓇᕐᓚᐊᓄ. ᑲᓇ ᑕᐅᒍᕐᒡ ᐃᓇᕐᒡ ᕐᐸᕐ
ᐊᓇᓇᕐᓄᒡᐱᓂ ᐊᓇᓇᕐᓚ ᐃᓚᐊᑉ ᕗᕐᓂ ᐊᓗᒡ ᑲᓇ ᕐᐸᕐᑉ
ᐅᓇᓚᒡᐱᓂ ᐊᓂᕐᒍ ᐊᓇᓂᓚᑦ ᑕᑉᓄᑲᓇᒡᒪ ᑕᐅᒍᔪᓇᓂᐊᒡᓚ,
ᑲᓇ ᐊᓇᓇᒍᓄ ᐊᑉᕐᐊᔪᑉ ᑲᐱᐊᕐᓯᒡᓚ ᐊᓂᓚ ᕐᒡᒍᐊᓄᑉ.
ᒪᓇᑕᓚ ᐃᓇᓇ ᐊᓂᒡᒍᓄᑉᐸᔪ ᕐᓂ ᐃᓇᓇ ᐅᐱᓂᐸᒍᒍᒡ.

ᒪᑯᒍᑉᐸᑲᐅᕐᒡ ᑕᐊᕐᒪᓚᐅᓄᒍᒡ. ᒪᑯᒍᐃ ᐃᓇᐃ ᓄᓚᐊᑕᐅᐱ
ᓇᕐᐊᓄᐸᑲᐅᐱᒪᓂᑲᑦ ᐱᓚᓄᐊᓄᕐᕐᑲᐅᐸᕐᒡᒍᒡᐱᐊᑦ ᑲᓄᒍᓄᑉ. ᒪᓇᓂ
ᐊᒡᓴᐊᓄᐃ ᕐᐸᕐ ᓄᐱᐊᕐᐊᓄ ᑕᐊᒡᒪᓇ ᐱᓚᐊᓂᐸᓄᒡᒍᒡ.

ᐊᓯᒍᓇᓄᒍ ᐅᐱᑕᐊᓂᕐᓚᐅᐸᒪ ᐊᑦᑕᒪ ᑐᒡᐱᕐᓚᐅᐸᒪ. ᑲᓇᒪᕐᑲ
ᐸᓄᑲᐅᐸᒡᓚᕐᑲ -- ᑲᓄᒪᑲᐅᐸᒡᒪᒡᒥ ᑐᓇᓯᓇᒡᓄᕐᓄ ᐊᓗᓄ

A drawing out of my mind.
Felt pen, 1970

ᐃᓯᒪᒐᓂ ᑎᑎᑐᒐᒃ
ᐃᒪᓕᒍ ᐊᓚᐅᑎᒍ ᑎᑎᑐᒐ, I970

I remember, there was a ship caught in the freeze-up in the ice just outside our camp. It was a beautiful ship, all white, and owned by Americans. They lived in their ship and the white men spent the time trapping for white fox. They used to send my brothers to the Bay in Cape Dorset to sell the skins and get the money. In the spring when break-up came, after my father died, the ship left.

ᑐᑯᓚᐅᓯᒪᕙᒃ ᓐᓇᑎᓂ ᐃᒃ ᓄᑲᒋᑐᒥ ᐃᑦ ᔨᑎᑐᒥ. ᑐᑯᑎᓄᒍ ᐊᐅᓚᔨᕙᒐ ᐅᒥᐊᕙᐊᑲᑎᓄᒍ ᓯᑯᒍᔭᒥ ᓐᓇᑕ ᓴᓂᑎᐊᑯᓄᐊᓂ. ᐅᒥᐊᕙᐊᑎᔭᐅᓯᓂ ᐊᒥᐊᑎᑲᒥᐅᓐᑦ. ᐅᒥᐊᒥᓂᓚᐅᓯᒪᕙ ᐊᒪᓄ ᑲᓄᓇᑦ ᒥᑭᒋᐊᓂᐊᑲᑕᓄᑎᒃ ᑎᑎᒐᓂᐊᓂ ᑲᑯᑕᔭᒥ. ᐊᓂᑯᓂ ᑭᔭᑲᐸᓚᐅᑐ ᑭᒐᓐᐊᑎᓯᓯᑎ ᓂᐅᕆᑎᒋᔭᐅᑯᔨᓯᑎ ᑎᑎᒐᓂᐊᔭᓂ ᑭᓇᐅᔭᑕᒍᑎᒋᓂᐊᓄᒋᑦ. ᐅᐱᒐᓴᐅᑎᓄᒍ ᓯᑯᐃᑐᐊᒪᑦ ᐊᑕᑕᒐ ᑐᑯᒐᓕᑎᓄᒍ, ᐅᒥᐊᕙᐊᒃ ᐊᐅᓚᓚᐅᓯᒪᕙᒃ.

After my father died, Ashoona's father came to get me on a dog team. Ashoona had told my brothers he would marry me; Ashoona and I used to be little children together. I don't remember how old I was when I married but girls got married very young then; now they are older. Ashoona's father took my mother and me on the dog team to Ikirasaq which is near Sakbuk, a one-day trip from Cape Dorset.

ᐊᑕᑕᒐ ᑐᑯᒐᓕᑎᓄᒍ, ᐊᒃᓯᓇᑉ ᐊᑕᑕᒐᓐ ᐊᐃᔭᐅᓚᐅᓯᒪᕙᒐ ᑭᒍᓯᑯᑦ. ᐊᒃᓯᓇᒃ ᐅᑲᓚᐅᓯᒪᕙ ᐊᓂᑯᓐ ᐅᕙᓂ ᓐᓕᐊᑕᒍᒪ ᓂᒐᓯᓂ; ᐊᒃᓯᓇᒃᓄ ᐱᐊᕋᐅᑲᑎᒋᐸᓚᐅᑐᒍ. ᐊᐅᓚᔨᒋᑐᒐ ᑲᓯᓂ ᐅᑭᐅᑲᓂᒪᒐᒪ ᐅᐃᑕᓯᒐ ᐃᓕ ᓂᕕᐊᓯᐊ ᒪᑯᑐᒪᑎᐅᓯᑎ ᐅᐃᑕᐸᓚᐅᑐᑦ ᑕᐃᓯᒪᓂ, ᒪᓇᓕ ᐃᓇᐅᓂᓴᐅᕙᓕᑐ. ᐊᒃᓯᓇᑉ ᐊᑕᑕᒐ ᐊᐃᓯᓚᐅᓯᒪᕙ ᐊᓇᓇᒐᓂᒃ ᐅᕙᓂᓄ ᑭᒍᓯᑯ ᐃᑭᕋᓴᒍ ᓴᒃᐸᐅ ᓴᓂᐊᓐ. ᐅᓄᒥ ᐊᑕᐅᓯᒥ ᐃᒋᕋᒋᐊᓕ ᑭᒐᓂ ᐱᓯᓂ.

We were married in the summer here in Cape Dorset. At that time of year all kinds of people from all the camps in the area used to come into Cape Dorset to see the ship

ᐅᐃᑕᓚᐅᓯᒪᕙᒐ ᐊᐅᔭᐅᑎᓄᒍ ᑕᕙᓂ ᑭᒐᓂ. ᑕᐃᓯᒪᓂᐅᑎᓄᒍ ᐊᕋᒍᑦ ᑭᓇᓕᒪᑯᑦ ᐃᓐᐃᑦ ᓇᑭᑐᐃᓇ ᓐᓇᓂ ᐱᕙ ᑭᒐᐃᑦ ᓴᓂᐊᓂᒥᐅᑦ ᑎᑭᐸᓚᐅᑐᑦ ᑭᒐᓐᑦ ᑕᑯᓂᐊᓯᑎ ᐅᒥᐊᕙᐊᒥᒃ ᓂᐅᕕᐊᓴᓂ ᐅᓯᒪ ᓂᐅᕕᐱᕕᐅᑉ ᐱᑯᑎᒋᓂ. ᑎᑭᑲᑕ ᐊᒥᓯᓚᐅᓯ

that would bring the supplies to the Bay. When we arrived
there were many people camped all over the hill where
the Hudson's Bay post is, and all around the bay. We
were married outside, by the flagpole near the Bay, by the
Anglican clergyman whose Eskimo name is 'Inutaquuq',
which means 'a new person'. All the people from the
camps were there.

Because Ashoona was an inland hunter, at our wedding
I had on caribou skin clothes – but they were just ordinary
clothes. Here in the Arctic we did not bother with special
dresses. But all through my married life, because Ashoona
was such a good hunter, he brought me beautiful skins –
all kinds of seal and caribou. Many women used to be
jealous of me because I had such lovely clothes.

For a short time after we married, we lived in Ikirasaq but,
before my first son was born, we moved to Akudluk
Island. It was a long journey but it took us only one day by
sail. It was windy and there was a good breeze on

ᒪᓇ ᐃᓄᐃᑦ ᑐᐱᕐᓕᖅᑐᒍᑎ ᓇᕐᑎᐃᓇᓕ ᑫᐅ ᓴᓇᐊᓂ
ᓂᐅᕙᐊᐃᐳᑦ ᓇᕐᑕᓂ ᐊᒪᓗ ᓯᕐᓚᓕᕐ. ᑲᑎᑕᑖᐃᐳᑕᕐᐱᓕᐊᒍᑦ
ᓯᕐᒥ ᓴᐊᓚᓴᐅᑎᑲᐊᒥ ᐃᐅᐃᐳᑦ ᓇᕐᐊᓂ ᐊᐅᐱᑐᐊᐱᒍ ᑲᑎᑎᑖ
ᐅᕐᓇ ᐃᐅᑎᑦ ᐊᑎᑲᐱᑐᐸᐊᓂᑲᔭᐱᒥ. ᐃᓄᒪᓕᑦ ᑐᐱᒪᐃᑐ
ᒪᓇ ᑕᐱᐊᓐᐃᐳᑎᐅᑦ. ᐊᑲᕐᐊᒃ ᓄᐅᒥ ᐊᔭᓇᕐᐊᐅᐱᓕᑦ
ᑲᑎᑲᑎᕐᓇ ᑐᑐᓇᑉ ᐊᓇᓯᕐᓕᑕᐅᕐᐸᓕᐊᕐ -- ᐃᓇ ᑐᑐᓯᐊ
ᐊᓇᓯᐊᐃᐳᑕᐅᕐᓕᐊᕐ. ᓚᓇ ᐃᓄᐃᑦ ᓄᐊᓄᒥ ᑲᓚᕐᐸᑲᐱᓕᐱᒍ
ᐊᓇᓯᓕᕐᐊᑲᕐᕐᐱᓴᖅ. ᐃᓇ ᑕᐊᒪᓕᓪ ᐅᐊᐱᓄᓕᓇ ᐊᐱᕐᓇ
ᐊᔭᓇᕐᐊᕐᑖᐱᓪᑕᐅᐳᑦ ᐅᓕᓕᐅᑉᕐᑖᐱᓪᑕᐅᐳᑦ ᑭᕐᓕᐊᑕᓇᕐᐱ
ᐱᐳᑖᐱ ᐱᑖᐱᓴᓂᓚ -- ᑲᓄᐊᑐᑖᐃᐱᓇ ᐊᕐᐱᕐᕐᓇ ᐊᓂᕐᓴ
ᑐᑐᓴᓇᓱ. ᐊᕐᒥ ᐊᕐᓇᐃᑦ ᐱᐊᓱᐸᕐᑖᐱᑦ ᐅᑲᓴ ᐱᐅᕐᐊᓴᓇ
ᐊᓇᒃᐸᐊᐳᒪᒪ.

ᑲᑎᑕᐅᑲᕐᒫᐱᓄᓚ, ᓄᐊᑲᐅᐳᐱᓕᐊᒍ ᐃᐱᕐᓴᕐ ᐃᓂ, ᐊᓕᐱᕐ
ᔭᐅᑕ ᐃᓴᐊᓄᓂ ᐃᐅᓕᑕᐅᑎᓇᐊᒍ, ᓄᑲᐅᐱᓕᐊᒍ ᐊᒍᓚᒍ. ᐊᒍᓂ
ᐊᕐᓴᑲᐅᐱᓕᐊᒍ ᐃᓇ ᐅᒃ ᓄᒥ ᐊᑕᐅᐱᕐ ᑭᕐᐊᓂ ᐅᕐᐊᑐᑲᐅᐱ
ᓚᐊᒍ. ᐊᓇᓴᓇᓇ ᐊᓇᕐᐅᔭᓄᑦ ᑯᕐᐱᐅᑎᒍᑦ. ᐊᐅᑐᐱᔭᓕ

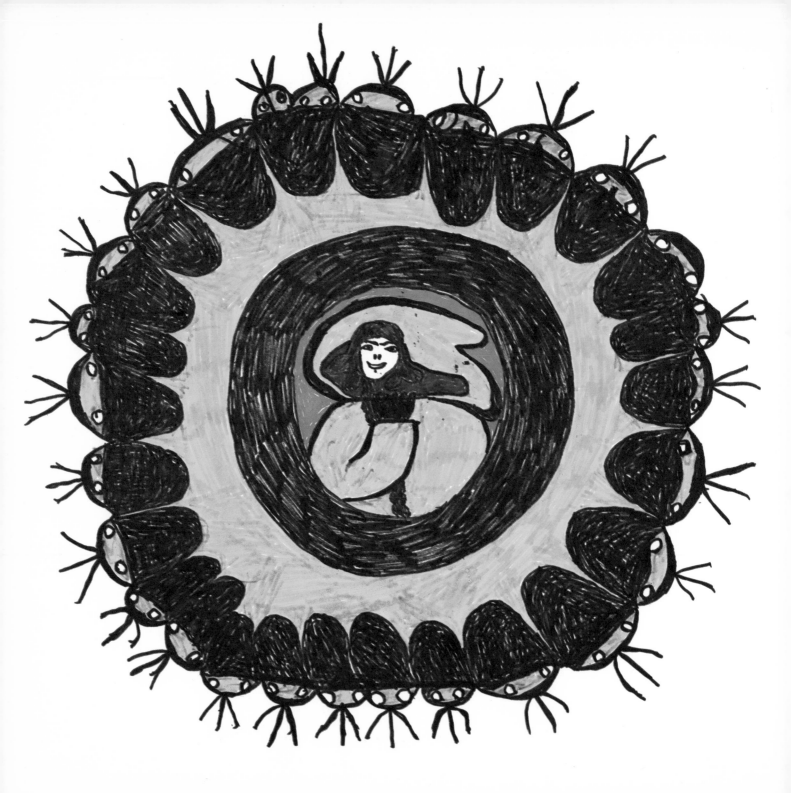

Safe in the tent.
Felt pen, 1970

ᐊᑕᕐᑐᒃ ᑐᐱᒥ
ᐃᒪᓪᒍ ᐊᓴᐅᖂᒍ ᑎᑎᑐᒃ, I970

our necks. I remember it was autumn and it was snowing
but there was no ice on the water. My husband's two
brothers and their families came with us and we were in
camp together for one year at Akudluk.

When Namoonie, my first son, was born, three women
held me. It was like that in the old times – there were
always women who helped. Afterwards, they would make
magic wishes for the child – that a boy should be a good
hunter, that a girl should have long hair, and that the
child should do well at whatever he was doing.

I don't know if it is easier to have babies in a hospital.
Ahalona! At any time it is hard. There is a saying, "It is
hard but it is well." I had 17 children – every year I
had a baby – and many of them died as little children.
In the Eskimo way, two sons were adopted, one by Peter
Pitseolak and one by another Eskimo couple, and
they died, too. Later, a daughter died from having a baby.
My living children are Namoonie, Kaka, Kumwartok,

ᐅᑭᐊᖅᐅᑎᓗᒍ ᑲᓗᓱᖐ ᐊᓗ ᓲᖅᒪᒥᑭᖏᓱᐊᔾᖐ ᐊᒪᖕ. ᐅᐊᒪ
ᖊᖐᒥ ᒪᖅᐊᑉ ᑭᑐᒪᒍ ᒪᓗᑎ ᐅᐸᓇ ᐊᖃᖕ ᐊᒪᓗ ᑐᐱᒃᒪᖐ
ᒥᓗᑎ ᐊᓯᒍᒥ ᐊᑐᐅᒥ ᐊᑯᓲᒥ. ᓇᐅᒪᓇᐃ, ᐊᒪᒉᒃᑯᑎᑎ
ᐃᓂᓕᑎᐅᔾᒪᐧ, ᐊᖃᓄᑦ ᐱᒪᓄ ᐊᖅᐧᓴᐅᓱᒪ. ᑕᐃᒪᐧᐸ
ᓴᐅᒪᓯ ᐅᖐᒪᐧᐅ -- ᐊᖃᐃ ᑕᐃᒪᒍᑦ ᐊᖅᐧᑎᒪᐅᑐᑦ.
ᐃᓂᓯᒪᓂᒪ ᐊᖐᖃᒍ ᐱᒍᓴᐅᖅᒍ ᐱᐊᒍᒪ ᓴᕐᑐᐅᒍ
ᐊᖃ ᓇᓯᐊᖃᐅᒍᓄ ᓯᖐᖐᐧᐸᑦ ᐊᒍᓇᐧᐊᖐᓂᐅᐧᖃᐅᒍ,
ᓂᐱᐊᖐᐧᐊᒍᐸ ᓄᐧᒍᒍᐧᖃᐅᒍ ᐊᒪᓗ ᑕᓇ ᐱᐊᖃ ᐱᖐᓂᒍᒍᒍ
ᖃᓇᑎ ᐊᓂᓕᖕ ᖃᓂᐊᓄᒥᓄᑦ.

ᖃᐅᖐᓯᑐᒪ ᐊᖃᐅᓱᖅᐅᑎᑎ ᐱᐊᒍᑲᑎᐊᖐ ᐊᓄᐊᐊᒥ. ᐊᖃᖐᐊ
ᐊᖃᖐᐊᒍ ᒪᐅᐊᒍ! ᖃᐅᒍᐊᓇ ᐊᖃᐅᒍᑐ. ᐊᓄᐊ ᐅᖃᖐᐧᐊᖃᒍᑐ,
ᐊᖃᐅᒍᑐ ᐊᓗ ᖃᐅᐊᑎᖐᐧᐊᒍ. ᐱᐊᒍᖃᖐᒪᒪᒪ I7-ᓂ
ᐊᒍᒍᑕᑦᓭ ᐱᐊᒍᖃᖐᒪᐧᐊᒪ ᐊᒪᓗ ᑐᐧᖐᒪᐧ ᐊᒥᖐᐊ ᐱᐊᒍᐧᐸᖐ
ᑎᖕ. ᐊᓂᑎ ᒪᐧᖕ ᑎᒍᐊᖃᐧᒪᐧᐧ, ᐊᖃᐧᖐ ᐱᐊ ᐱᖐᐅᒍ
ᐊᒪᓗ ᐊᐧᐊᑕ ᑎᒍᐊᖃᒍᐧᐧᓄ ᐊᓇᓄ ᓄᖃᓄᓄ ᐊᒪᓗ ᑕᖐᐧ
ᑕᒪᖐᖕ ᑐᖐᒪᐧᖐᐧᖃᐅᖐ. ᖐᐊᖂᑐ ᐸᓄᓇ ᑐᖐᐅᑐ ᐱᐊᒍᒪ.
ᐱᐊᒍᖕ ᐊᓄᐧ ᒪᓇ ᓇᐅᖐᓇᐃ, ᖃᖃ, ᖂᒪᑿᐊᖃᖕ, ᑭᒍᐊᑦ,

Kiawat, Ottochie and Nawpachee. Among those who are living I have only one daughter, Nawpachee. Except for Kaka who lives in camp in the old way, they all live here in Cape Dorset, and now I live with Kumwartok and his wife.

On Akudluk Island, where Namoonie was born, there was good hunting. There were no caribou but there were polar bear, walrus and seal. But I did not care for Akudluk — my relatives were all around Cape Dorset, and it was too hard to get the white man's food from the Bay. We had no tea, only meat. After a year we went back to Cape Dorset for a short time, and then to Ikirasaq where we were in camp with Peter Pitseolak and lots of families. I don't remember them all or how many there were; in those days we didn't bother counting people.

But my husband used to be a very busy man with the hunting and he didn't like to live with other people. There are many days in the year and we moved many times — maybe ten times a year. We would often camp at Natsilik,

ᐅᑐᑭ, ᖃᐸᕐᐸᓱ. ᑕᑯᓇᓂ ᐃᓄᕠᓇ ᐊᑕᐅᕐᒥ ᑭᕐᐊᓂ ᐸᓂᑲᑐᒐ, ᖃᐸᕐᒥ. ᑫᑫ ᑭᕐᐊᓂ ᐃᕈᓘᑤᕐᒄᕐᒋᑐ ᐅᕐᕐᐊᐅ ᓂᑐᑦ ᐃᓄᕚ.ᐃᓱᐊᓴ ᑕᒪᓂ ᑭᒥᕠᐅᒐᕚ ᐊᒪᓴ ᒪ ᐃᐊᕚ ᖃᓂᕠᐅᕚᒥ ᓂᕐᐊᓂᓱ ᐊᓇᕟᕐᒪ.

ᐊᒄᓘᒥ, ᑕᐃᕠᓂ ᓇᒄᐃᓇ ᐃᓄᕐᑕᐅᕐᒫᕚ ᑕᐃᕠᓂ ᐅᒮᕠᑭᕚ ᓴᐅᑐ. ᑐᑐᑳᕠᓚᓂ ᐃᓴ ᓴᓄᕠᓇ, ᐊᑦᐊᓂ ᓇᕈᓱ. ᐃᓴ ᐊᒄᓄᕝ ᐱᐅᕠᓄᕚᕟᒪ -- ᐃᓴᕝ ᐃᓱᐊᓂ ᕠᓗᓇᐅᓚᕟ ᐊᒪᓱ ᐊᕈᐊᕈᓱᓇ ᕯᓱᓇᕟ ᓇᕕᓇᕟ ᓄᐅᐊᐊᓴᓇᒐ. ᓂᕟᑳᐅᕟᑐᒄ ᑕᐃᕠᓂ ᓇᕕᒥ ᑭᕐᐊᓂ. ᐊᖃᒄ ᐊᑕᕐᕝ ᐊᓄᒐᒪ ᐅᑎᕠᓇᐅᑐᒄ ᕕᓱ ᕕᑕ ᑕᐃᕠᓇᕐᑕᕝ, ᐊᒪᓱ ᑕᐊᒪ ᐃᕕᕠᑕᒐ ᓇᕟᐅᑐᑥᕝ ᑕᐃᕠᓂ ᑐᐱᕠᓚᕠᓂᕠᓇᓱᕠᑥ ᐱᕝ ᐱᕈᐅᕠᒥ ᐊᒪᓱ ᐊᕟᕈᐊᓱᓇ ᐃᓴᕟᓂ. ᐊᕚᓇᕟᕝᕟᕝ ᐃᓱᐊᓂ ᐊᒪᓱᓇ ᕗᐅᕠᕠᓇ ᒪᕠᓂ ᐊᕚᓇᕟᑐᒪ, ᑕᐊᕯᕠᒥ ᕝᓂᕟᕠᐊᕠᕝ ᕗᕝᕟᓇᕟᒐᕟ.

ᕢᕚᓇᓇ ᐅᐊᒪ ᐊᕝᕟᐊᓱ ᓄᕗᕠᕚᐊᕟᕝᕟᑳᐅᕠᓚᕮ ᐊᑤᓇᕟᐊᕟᓇ ᑕᐊᒪ ᐃᐱᕝᕚᕟᑐᒄᑐ ᓄᐊᕟᕯᕚᕝᐊᕝ ᐊᕟᕟᓇ ᐃᓇᓂ. ᐅᕝ ᓱᐊ ᐊᕠᕟᐊᕜᐅᕟᕚᕝ ᐊᕚᒄᒥ ᐊᒪᓱ ᓄᕢᕟᕝ ᐊᕠᕟᕚᕟᕝᕝ -- ᐃᕝᕝ IO ᑯᕜᐊᓱᕝ ᐊᕚᒄᒥ ᓄᕝᕝᕚᕝᕝᕝᕝ. ᑐᐱᕝᕚᕚᕝ ᓇᕟᕟᒥ,

Woman and dogs.
Engraving, 1967

ᐊᒃᓇᒃ ᑭᒥᓗ
ᐅᑯᓯᓴᔭᒥ ᓴᓇᒍᐊᓚ, I967

a place about a week's journey from Cape Dorset, near many lakes. It had the most beautiful drinking water, the most beautiful water I have ever found. We often went to Natsilik to hunt fish; and at Natsilik, too, there were many geese. Later on, white people we met from the Department of Transport used to go there, too, and some of them called it 'Ashoona's Land'. Today, sometimes Namoonie still goes to Natsilik – but now he flies by plane.

ᑕᐃᑯᓚ ᐱᓇᓯᐊᒍᓯᓕᒪᒥ ᐃᒋᕋᒋᐊᓕ ᑭᓚᓂ ᐱᓯᓂ ᑕᓯ ᐊᒥᓯ ᓴᓂᐊᓂ. ᑕᐃᑲᓂ ᐱᐅᓂᐸᒥ ᐃᒥᕋᓴᑕᑲᑐ ᐃᒥᒥᒃ. ᐱᐆᓂᐸᒃ ᐃᒥᒃ ᑕᑯᓚᐅᓯᒪᔭᓕᒪᕋᓂ ᐃᒥᓯᐊᑲᓂᐸ. ᓇᓯᓕᒎᐸᓚᐅᑐᒍ ᐃᑲᓄᓂᐊᑎᐊᓯᑕ, ᐊᒪᓗᑕᐅ ᑕᐃᑲᓂ ᓇᑦᓯᓕᒥ ᐊᒥᓯᓂᒃ ᓂᓕᑲᐸᓚᐅᒥᔪ. ᓯᐊᕆᓕᑎᓗᒍ ᑲᓗᓇᓗ ᑲᑎᓕᓚᐅᓯᒪᔪᒍ ᑕᑯᐊ ᓇᓕᑎᑯᓂ ᐃᑲᓇᐃᔭᑐ ᑕᐃᑯᓚᑲᑕᓚᐅᓯᒪᔪᑕᐅ ᐊᒪᓗ ᐃᓚᒋᓄ ᑕᐃᔭᐅᕙᓚᐅᑐᒃ ᐊᒃᓯᓇᑉ ᓄᓇᓚ. ᒪᓇ ᐃᓚᓂᑯᑦ ᓇᐅᒥᓇᐃ ᓯᓕ ᓇᓯᓕᒎᑲᑕᐅᒃ ᐃᓚ ᒪᓇᓕ ᑲᓚᑕᓯᑯᑦ ᑎᒥᑲᑕᓕᐅᒃ.

Sometimes we went to the islands near Cape Dorset for seal and walrus. Spring and autumn are the best times for this kind of hunting.

ᐃᓚᓂᑯᑦ ᑭᓚᐃᑦ ᓴᓂᐊᓂ ᓄᓇᑲᐸᓚᐅᑐᒍᑦ ᓇᓯᓯᐅᑎᐊᓯᑕ, ᐊᐃᕕᓯᐅᑎᐊᓯᒪᓯᑕᓗ. ᐅᐱᓚᓴᒥ ᐅᑭᐊᒃᓴᒥᓗ ᐱᐅᓂᐸᒍᕙᓗᓂ ᑕᒪᑐᒎᓚ ᐊᕗᒋᒋᑐᓂᒃ ᐊᒍᓇᓯᐊᓗᓂ.

Both in summer and winter we used to move a lot. In summer there were always very big mosquitoes. I have made many drawings of moving camp in summertime and I always put in the mosquitoes. I do not like insects.

ᑕᒪᐃᓂ ᐊᐅᔭᑯᑦ ᐅᑭᐊᑯᓗ ᐊᐅᓚᒋᓇᐸᓚᐅᑐᒍᑦ ᐊᒥᓯᕕᓯᑕ. ᐊᐅᔭᑯ ᑕᐃᒪᓚ ᐊᒋᔪᐸᓗᓂ ᑭᑐᑎᐊᑲᐸᓚᐅᑐ. ᑎᑎᑐᔭᓯᒪᔪᓚ ᐊᐅᓚᑐᓂᒃ ᓄᓇᒎᑦ ᐊᐅᔭᐅᑎᓗᒍ ᐊᒪᓗ ᑕᐃᒪᓚ ᐃᓕᓯᕙᓯᓚ ᑭᑐᑎᐊᓂᒃ. ᐱᐅᓴᔭᒋᑐᓚ ᑯᐱᕆᓂᒃ.

Sometimes, when we camped in a place for the first time, we would put up an 'inukshuk'. My father and Ashoona

ᐃᓚᓂᑯ ᑐᐱᓯᒪᓯᑕ ᑐᐱᓯᒪᕕᑎᓂ ᓯᕗᓕᒥ, ᐃᓕᕗᑲᑕᓚᐅᓯᒪᔪᒍᑦ ᐃᓄᒃᓯᓂ. ᐊᑕᑕᓚ ᐊᒃᓯᓇᓗ ᑕᒪᒥ ᐊᑭᓯᐃᕙᓚᐅᑐᒃ

Woman with geese.
Engraving, 1967

ᐋ�b ᖏᐊᑯ ᐋᒡᓗ ᓄᑲᓄᑲ
ᐅᑯᖲᕼᕓᒥ ᑎᑎᑐᒪᒪ, 1967

both built them from time to time, and Kumwartok built one a few weeks ago when he camped for the first time at a new place near Akudluk Island. A few years ago people from the Co-op built inukshuks above Cape Dorset, and these reminded me of the ones we used to make and I drew some for the prints.

In the old days we had different kinds of housing for the different seasons. We had the igloo, the 'kaamuk', which is a tent-hut, and the summer tents.

In winter I didn't mind whether we had an igloo or a kaamuk so long as we had a shelter for our family.

To build an igloo you have to have the right snow, but what kind of snow I don't know. Men built the igloos. I remember when I was a little girl I once built an igloo myself, but it was a funny-looking igloo – skinny and tall! Perhaps they take an hour to build, but in those days we didn't have watches. It is better to know the time. It used to be okay

ᑐᐱᐊᐳᓄ ᐃᓄᑲᑕᐅᖕᑲᑐᑐ ᐋᒡᓄ ᑯᒡᑐᒍ ᐃᓄᑲᑕᐅᑕᑐᖲ
ᐱᓄᑲᑐᐳᔅ ᐊ�²²ᒪᑐ ᓇᑲᖢᑲᑎᓄᒪ ᑐᐊᕂᖢᒪᕂᐋᑕ᷍ᑕᖄ
ᓄᕉᒪ ᓇᓇᕉᒪ ᐋᑯᓇᕍ ᕼᓇᐋᐱᓄᖏ. ᐊᕍᒍᐃ ᐊᑲᕂᕂᑐ ᐊᓇᒍᕉ
ᐳᕂᑐᒍ ᐃᓄᐃᑕ ᑯᑐᐊᕙᑐᑕ ᐃᓄᑲᕂᑕᐅᑐᕼᖢᕋ ᕘᓯᐃᑕ
ᓇᕈᓇ ᐊᒡᓄ ᑕᑯᐊ ᐃᑲᐊᒍᑎᕂᑐᕒᕀ ᐃᓄᑲᕂᑲᐊᕍᑲᑕᕂᑕᖄ
ᑕᐋᒪ ᐃᕙᕉᕈᒃ ᑎᑎᑐᕼᑕᐅᑐᒪ ᐃᕙᕂᖏ ᐊᕀᕂᑐᒪᕂ.

ᐅᕂᕈᐊᑐᕉᒍ ᐊᕼᕂᕂᑐᒍ ᐃᕙ ᕊᑲᕂᕀᑕᐅᑐᖏ ᐅᕉᐅ ᐅᕌᑯᒍ
ᐊᐅᖢᒍ. ᐊᐅᑎᒥ ᐃᕙ ᕽᓇᕉᕀᑯᖢᕽ, ᕙᒍᒥ ᑐᕂᕀᐳᓇ ᓇᕉᒥ,
ᐊᒡᓄ ᐊᐅᖢᕀᑯ ᑐᕼᕉᑐᕉᖢᖄᑕ.

ᐅᕉᐅ ᕙᓇᕂᖢᕀᑯᐅᑐᕂᑐᒪ ᕒᕂᒥ ᐊᐅᒥ ᐃᕙ ᕽᕼᕉᕀᕙᕀᑲᐅᑕᕂᑕ
ᐅᕾᖢᓇ ᕙᒍᕉᕀᑕᕀᑕ ᐊᕒᖄᕙᖢ ᐅᕉᒍᑎᕙᕀᑲᐅᑐᕒᕀᑕ ᕼᐅᕂᑎᖏ.

ᐊᐅᑎᒥ ᐃᕙ ᕽᓇᕉᕀᑐᓇ ᓇᕏᒍᒥ ᐊᐅᒥᕙ ᐊᑐᕀᐊᕙᕒᕀ ᐊᐃ
ᕙᓇᕂᐅᕀᕍᒪ ᐊᐅᑎ ᕙᕙᕂᕒᒍᕀᕉ. ᐊᒍᕀᕉ ᐃᕙ ᕽᓇᕉᕀᕙᐅᕂᕎᕀᕌᕌᕂᑕ.
ᐊᐅᕍᖄᕂᕍ ᓇᕂᐋᖢᕀᐊᕉᕂᕍ ᐃᕙᓇᕂᖢᕍᐅᐳᕍᕂᕀᕌᕍᕂᕌ ᐊᑕᐳᕍᐊᕂᕌ
ᕘᕙᐃᕂᓇ ᐃᕙ ᕽᓇᕂᖢᕀᑯᕀᕽᕙᕀᑲᐅᕂᕌᕂᑕᕀᕂ -- ᐊᕂᕍᕀᐊᕂᖄᕂᕘᕀ
ᑕᐅᕒᕀᐊᐅᕂᕍᕀᖄ! ᐃᕙᕀᑲ ᕙᑯᕀᕀᑎᕒᒍᕂᒪᕒᕀ ᐃᕙ ᕽᓇᕂᖢᕀᑯᕀᕍᕀᖢᕀᕙᑐᕀᑕ
ᐃᕙᕂᕂᓇ ᑕᕼᕉᒪᕀᕎᐳᕀᑎᕂᕂᖢᒍ ᐅᐳᕂᖢᕀᕙᕀᑲᐅᑐᕒᕀᓇᕀᑕ ᑕᕂᕍᕂᕎᕀᕙᕀ. ᕽᕌᕀᖢᕂᕍᐅ

It was good to have a new snow house.
Felt pen, 1970

ᐃᓗᕕᒐᑕᑲᒥᒋᐊᒥᒃ ᐱᐅᕙᓚᐅᑐᒃ
ᐃᒪᓕᒧ ᐊᓚᐅᑎᒧ ᑎᑎᑐᒐ, 1970

Around the igloo.
Engraving, 1964

ᐃᒃ ᓗᕕᒐᐅᑉ ᓯᓚᑕᓂ
ᐅᑯᓯᓴᔪᒥ ᑎᑎᑐᒐ, 1964

without clocks, but it is okay with clocks, too. Now I am used to watching the time. The igloo would last all winter but often it would melt and drip inside from the heat of the kudlik. We used to dig a trench around the base to catch the water, and the women would scrape the soft snow from the walls inside with their 'ulus', the women's knives.

It was good to have a new snow house built because they were easy to clean – and very clean. But sometimes, if it was windy, the wind blew holes in the snow house, so perhaps the kaamuk was more comfortable.

To make the kaamuk, we would put up a tent and line the inside with wood. Between the tent and the wood we would put little bushes – sometimes blueberry bushes – to make it warm. I remember when Kumwartok, my son, got married. He and his wife were building the hut and she was carrying the bushes on her back. They were too heavy for her and she fell down, covered in bushes. They laughed. They were happy, building the hut together.

ᑎᓗᒍ ᑲᓯᒍᒪᒪᒐ ᑲᐅᔪᒪᒋᐊᓴ. ᑲᓄᐃᐸᓚᐅᒋᒥᔭ ᓯᑭᒍᔪᑲᒐᑕ ᐃᓚ ᑲᓄᐃᒋᒥᔭᒃ ᓯᑭᒍᔪᑲᑐᓂ. ᒪᓇᓕ ᓯᒋᐅᓯᓯᒪᓕᐳᒐ ᑲᐅᔪᒪᒋᐊᓴ ᑲᓯᒍᒪᒪᒐ. ᐃᒃ ᓗᕕᒐ ᐅᑭᐅᓕᒪᒥ ᐊᑐᒍᓇᐸᓚᐅᑐ ᐃᓚᓂ ᑭᓯᐊᓂ ᐃᒃ ᓗᕕᒐ ᐊᐅᐸᓚᐅᑐ ᑯᓯᕙᑐᓂᑐ ᐃᑐᐊᒍᑦ ᑯᓕᐅᑉ ᐅᑯᓂᒐᓄ. ᐳᐊᑎᔪᐸᓚᐅᑐᒍ ᐃᓗᕕᒐ ᑲᕕᒥᒧᑲᐃᓯᑕ ᐃᒥᑎᑕᐃᓕᓯᒍ ᐊᒪᓗ ᐊᒃᓇᐃᑦ ᐱᔪᐃᕙᓚᐅᑐ ᐊᐳᑎᔪᐃᓯᑎ ᐊᑭᑐᒥ ᐊᑭᓇᒥ ᐃᒃ ᓗᕕᒐᐅᑉ ᐃᑐᐊᓂ ᐅᑐᒥᓄ. ᐱᐅᕙᓚᐅᔭᔭ ᓄᑕᒥ ᐃᒃ ᓗᕕᒐᑕᑲᒥᐅᒋᐊᓴ ᓴᓗᒪᓴᒋᐊᒐ ᐊᑲᐅᕙᓚᐅᔭᒪᑕ, ᐊᒪᓗ ᓴᓗᒪᔭᐸᓗᓯᑎᒃ. ᐃᓚᓂᑯᑦ ᑭᓯᐊᓂ ᐊᓄᕆᓚᒐᐃᒪᑦ ᓯᐳᐸᓗᑎ ᑭᓚᒋ ᐊᐳᒥ ᐃᒃ ᓗᕕᒐᒥ ᑕᐃᒪ ᐃᒪᑲ ᑕᓇ ᑲᒧᑦ ᐃᓯᐊᓂᓴᐅᕙᑐᕕᓂᒃ.

ᑲᒧᓕᐅᓯᑕ ᑐᐱᓕᐅᐸᓚᐅᑐᒍ, ᐊᒪᓗ ᑐᑭᒧᐊᑐᓂᒃ ᐃᑐᐊᒍᑦ ᑭᔭᑕᓯᓯᒍ. ᐊᑯᓂᒐᒍᑦ ᑐᐱᐅᑉ ᑭᔭᑐ ᓄᓇᕆᔪᐱᑕᓯᓯᒍ -- ᐃᓚᓂ ᐸᐅᒐᑯᕕᓂ ᓄᓇᕆᔪᑕᓯᓯᒍ ᐅᑯᓯᓂᐊᒪᑦ. ᐊᐅᓚᓯᔭᒐ ᑕᐃᓯᒪᓂ ᐃᒃᓂᒐ ᑯᒧᐊᑐ, ᓄᓕᐊᑕᒐᒥ ᓄᓕᐊᒐᓗ ᐃᒃ ᓗᓕᐅᓚ ᐅᓯᒪᔭ ᑲᒧᒥ ᑕᐃᒪ ᓄᓕᐊᒐ ᓇᒪᓚᐅᓯᒪᔭ ᓄᓇᕆᓂ. ᓄᓇᕆᓂ ᓇᒪᑕᒥᓂ ᐅᑯᒪᐃᓴᓗᐊᒐᒥ ᓇᒪᑕᒥᓄ ᐸᓚᑎᑕᐅᓚᐅᓯᒪᔭ ᒪᑐᓗ ᓂ ᓄᓇᕆᓂᒃ. ᐃᓚᓚᐅᓯᒪᔭ ᐃᔭᓚᐅᓯᒪᔭ. ᑯᕕᐊᓯᐸᓚᐅᑐ, ᐃᒃ ᓗᓚᐅᓗᑎ ᑲᒧᒥ ᑲᑐᔪᓯᑎᒃ.

In summer I lived in a great big
sealskin tent (detail).
Felt pen, 1970

ᐊᐳᏝᒡ ᐅᓴᕐ ᑭᓯᓛᓂ ᑐᒪᕐ᙭ᑕᐅᑐᒪ
ᐃᓚᒼᒍ ᐊᒼᐅᏁᒍ ᑎᑎᒪᒪ, I970

In the kaamuk we put a window. We made the window
from the intestine of the whale. We would clean it and blow
it up with air and hang it up to dry in long pieces. This
made a good window. It was also from the whale intestine
that we made sails for the sealskin boats.

In the summers before I was married I lived in a great
big sealskin tent made from the 'udjuk', the square-flipper
seal. These tents were so large they used to be used by
two families. Inside there was a great room and usually
the children slept on the 'kilu', the sleeping platform, at
the back of the tent and far away from the door. The
grown-ups slept just in front of the kilu on the 'ilukatigit',
which means 'both sides of the tent'. This was a sleeping
platform for two families or four grown-ups.

The sealskin tent was changed every summer because
it would dry out and then it was very hard to use. I used to
see my mother make these tents. She would scrape
the udjuk three times with the ulu and sew the skins on

Ꮟᒍᒥ ᐃᑫ ᓬᑕᐅᒥᐸ ᐃᓚᕐᕐᐅ᙭ᑕᐅᑐᒍ. ᐃᓚᕐᕐᐅ᙭ᑕᐅᒪ ᐊᑐ᙭ᐸ
ᐅᑐᒍ ᑭᓬᓬᐅᐸ ᐊᑭᐊᒍᓬᓂ.ᓵᓬᕐᕙᕐᐅᒍ ᐊᓬᓬᑕᐅᐸᕐᐅᒍ
ᕐᓴᒥ ᑿᓬᑕᓬᕐᐅᒍ ᕙᓂᕐᐊᓂᕐᐅᒍ ᑕᕐᕐᐅᑎᐅᓂᓬᒍ. ᑕᓇ
ᐃᓬᑯᕐᐊᒍ᙭ᑕᐅ᙭ᑿᒍ. ᐊᓬ᙭ᑕᕿ ᑭᓬᓬᐅᐸᕐ ᐊᑭᐊᒪᓬ᙭ᑿ
(ᐃᕿᕐᓬᓂ) ᑎᕐᓯᐅᑕᕐᐅ᙭ᑕᐅᒍᒍ ᑭᕐᓬ ᐅᕐᐊᑎᓬ᙭ ᑎᕐᓯᐅᑕ
ᕐᐊᑎᕐᕐᓂᕐ.

ᐊᐳᏝᒡ ᐅᐃᑕᕿᐅᑎᓬᑕ ᐊᓬᕐᕿᕿᐅᕐᓬ᙭ᒍ ᐊᕿ᙭᙭ᓬᕐ ᑭᕿᕐ
ᐅᕐᕐ ᑭᓯᓛᓂ. ᑕᑕ᙭ ᑐᐃᕐ ᐊᕿ᙭᙭ᓬ᙭᙭ᑕᐅ᙭ ᐊᑐᑕᐅ᙭ᑿ
ᒪᑭᐃᓬᕐ ᑭᒍᓬ᙭ᓬ. ᐃᓬ᙭ᓂᕐ ᐊᕿ᙭᙭ᓬᕐᕐᒪᕐ ᐃᓬᕿᓬᓂᕐ ᐊᓬ᙭
ᐱᕿᒍᐃ ᑭᓬ᙭ᓂᕐ ᕐᓂ᙭ᓬᑎ ᑭᓬᕐᐅᑕᐅ᙭᙭ᑿ. ᐃᓬᐃ ᐃᐅᓬᑎ
ᕐᓂ᙭᙭ᑿ ᑭᓬ᙭ ᕙᓬᓂᕐ ᑭᕿᓬᓂᕐ. ᐃᑫ ᓬᑭᓂᕐᕐᓂ ᕐᓂᑭᓂᕐᐊ
ᐅ᙭᙭ᑿ ᒪᑭᐃᓬᓂ ᑭᒍᓬ᙭ᓂᕐ ᐅ᙭ᓬᓂᕐ ᕐᑕᓬᓂᕐ ᐃᓬᓬᓂᕐ.

ᓂᕐᐅ᙭ ᑭᕿᓬ ᑐ᙭ᐃᑫ ᐊᕿᕐᐱᕐᐊᑫ᙭᙭ᑿᕐ ᐊᐳᏝᑕᓬᕐ ᕙᓯ᙭ᓬᓯᕐ
ᐊᕿᒪ ᐊᓬ᙭ ᐊᑭᐅᕐᑐᒪᕐᐊᒍ᙭ᓂᕐ ᐊᑐᑎᐊᒪᕐ. ᑕᑭᓇ᙭᙭ᑕᐅᑐᒪ
ᐊᕙᕙᕿ᙭ ᑕᐃᓬᐊᑐᒪ ᑐ᙭ᑕᐅᑐᒪᒪ. ᐅ᙭ᕐᐊᕿᑿᐊᕐᓂᕐ ᓵᑭᕿᕐᓂᕐ

Talilayu who keeps the sea animals
away from the hunters.
Felt pen, ca. 1967

ᑕᓕᓛᕈᖅ ᐃᓗᐱᑦ ᐅᒪᔪᕐᓂᖅ ᐅᒪᔪᓄᐊ
ᑎᓄᑦ ᐱᖦᐅᒍᓇᐅᕐᑕᓗ ᐊᓚᒡᓗ ᐊᖃᐅᑎ
ᒍᑦ ᑎᑎᕐᑕ, 1967 ᐅᑎᓗᒍ

We used to hang up the intestine
of the whale in long strips to dry.
Felt pen, ca. 1967

ᑭᓚᒪᐊᑦ ᐊᓇᓗᐊᕐᓂᖅ ᐸᖕᕐᔅᑲᐅᑦᔭᒍ
ᐊᓚᒡᓗ ᐊᖃᐅᑎᓗ ᑎᑎᕐᑕ,
1967 ᐅᑎᓗᒍ

the ground. These skins could dry out very quickly, too, so damp moss would be brought from the tundra to cover them as she worked.

The first year I was married I made a sealskin tent just for our family. I made only this one because, at the time, my mother used to stay in turns in our camp and in the camps of her sons. She would help me with all the sewing. Every year she made us a tent. Then, when I had four children, they began to sell canvas at the Bay. Ashoona was always able to buy canvas and so, after this, I made canvas tents. The last tents I made were for Jim Houston when he was here. One summer a group of white people – I think they were the first tourists – came and spent all summer camping here outside Cape Dorset. Eskimo families went and lived with them. I made about six tents.

In the old way, of course, women also made the boats. I never sewed for a sealskin boat but I used to sew for the

ᐅᐦᏟᎢ ᐱᒪᕐᐊᕐᓂ ᐅᓲᕐᓄᑦ ᒥᒐᒪᕐᑯᓗ ᑭᕐ.ᑕᑐᐊ ᑭᕐᑦ
ᐸᓂᕐᑐᑎᕐᐊᐱᒍᓂᒪᕐᔪᑐᐱ ᑕᐅᒪ ᐸᑐᕐᐅᑭ ᓄᓇᕐᔪᕐᑭ ᐊᑐᓐᑎ
ᕐᐸᓄᐅ ᓄᓇᕐᔪᕐᒥᕐ ᓂᕐᒥ ᓗᑐᕐᔫ ᑕᐱᓐᐊ ᐱᐊᕐᐸᓄᐅᑎᕐᑭ.

ᕐᐅᓄᐸᕐᒥ ᐊᔅᔫᒥ ᐅᐃᓄᑭᕐᑎᐅᕐᒪ ᓇᕐᕐᒥ ᑭᕐᒥ ᐅᐊᑎᐅᓴᐅᕐᐱ
ᒪᕐᒪ ᐳᐅᒧᕐᔫᑎ ᑭᕐᐊᓄ ᐅᐱᕐᓄᓂ. ᑕᓇ ᓴᐊᓚᐱᕐᒪᕐᑭ
ᑭᕐᐊᓄ ᑕᐱᕐᒪᓄᐅᓐᔫᒍ ᐊᐊᓇᒪ ᐅᐱᐸᓂᕐᑭ ᓚᐱᕐᔫᒪᕐᒪ ᐊᒪᔫ
ᐊᕐᓄᕐᑭ ᐅᐊᕐᓄᕐᐱᕐᐊᓄ. ᐊᕐᐊᕐᑭ ᓐᓗᐅᕐᔫᕐᒥᕐᑭ ᓈᕐᒪᕐᓴᒐᓄ.
ᐊᔅᔫᑕᒪᕐ ᐅᐱᕐᐅᕐᑭ ᓐᓗᐅᕐᔫᕐᕐ ᐅᑭᕐᓄᕐ. ᑕᐱᒪ ᑕᐅᕐᒪᓄ
ᕐᑎᓄᕐᑭ ᐱᐊᔅᕐᐸᓐᔫᒪ, ᐅᐱᕐᔨᒥᕐ ᓄᐅᐊᐊᕐᑭᕐᕐᐅᕐᔫᕐᐅᕐ
ᓄᐅᐱᐱᒥᒪ. ᐊᕐᐊᔫᕐᓇᕐ ᑕᐱᕐᐱᒪ ᓄᐅᐱᓄᕐᐸᕐᐸᓄᐅᑭ ᐊᒪᔫ ᑕᐱᒪ
ᐅᐱᔫᕐᑭᕐᐅᐊᒪ ᐅᐱᕐᐅᐸᕐᕐᐅᔫᑎ. ᐳᐅᑭᒥᕐ ᐅᐱᕐᐊᒪ ᓴᓄᑭ
ᐱᐱᒪ ᓴᐅᕐᐅ ᓴᐊᕐᑭᕐ ᔫᕐᑕᐱᐱ - ᐅ ᑕᒪᓄᐅᓄᐅ. ᐊᐅᕐᔫᑭ
ᐸᔫᓄᕐ ᐱᐸᑐᕐᒥᕐᐅ ᓐᑭᕐᐊᐱᕐᔫᕐ ᑕᒪᐅᒪ ᕐᐅᓄᐸᐅᑎᕐᐅᕐᔫᒥᕐ
ᓄᐅᔫᔫᕐᑭᑎᕐᑭᕐ - ᐅᓐᑭᕐᒥᕐ ᑕᒪᓄᐱᐅᕐᔫᕐᕐ ᐊᕐᐱᕐᓄᒪ ᐅᐱᕐᔫᑎ
ᑕᒪᓄ ᐱᑭᐱᕐᑭ ᐱᕐᒪ. ᐊᓄᒥᕐ ᐱᐅᓂᕐᓄ ᐊᒪᐊᐅᐸᕐᐅᔫᕐᑭᕐ
ᐅᐱᕐᒪᑭᐅᑎᕐᕐᐊᐅᕐᒥᕐ. ᐅᐱᕐᐅᐸᐅᕐᔫᒥᕐᑭ ᐱᐱᕐᔫᒍᔫᕐᓄᕐᑭ.

ᐅᐸᕐᐊᐱᓄᐅᕐ, ᕐᐱᐅᒪᕐ, ᐊᕐᓇᐊᐅᐸ ᒥᕐᐱᐊᐅᕐᔫᕐ.
ᒥᕐᑕᐅᕐᔫᕐᑭᕐᔫᑎᒥᕐ ᓇᕐᐸᕐ ᑭᕐᒪᓄ ᐅᒥᐊᕐ ᐱᕐᒥ ᑭᕐᐊᓄ

We would sew covers for kayaks with
sinew from the caribou leg muscle.
Coloured pencil and felt pen,
ca. 1967

ᖃᔭᐅᐸᒐᓴᑦ ᑐᑐᑦ ᓂᕈᒥᐅᖕᐱᒃ ᐃᕝᔪᖃᐸ
ᓚᕈᔪᑕ ᑕᖃᓴᓂ ᐋᓄᑎᓄᑦ ᐋᓗ
ᐃᓚᒥᓱ ᑎᑎᑐᒪ, I967 ᐅᑎᔪᒧ

kayaks. In the old days, usually the women would row
the sealskin boat and the men would go in the kayaks.
In one drawing, I have shown the women's boat towing
a kayak. If it became rough they would take the kayak-man
aboard. In this print, all around the boats are little pests.
What are they doing there? It is their business to be there.
Did Eskimos believe in spirits and pests and monsters?
Maybe they did. In the old days there was much to fear.

In the old days I was never done with the sewing. There
were the tents and the kayaks, and there were all the
clothes which were made from the different skins – seal,
caribou and walrus. From skins we also made cups for
drinking and buckets for carrying water. And when we
caught geese we used to make brooms for cleaning from
the wings which we bound together. If we had enough
brooms we would throw the wings away.

As soon as I was finished sewing one thing, I was always
sewing another. Sometimes, when I was very busy with

ᒥᕐ�<ᓇᐅᑐᒪ. ᐅᔭᕐᐊᑎᓄᒍ ᐋᖃᓄᐊᑦ ᐸᑭᔭᐅᑐ ᓇᕐᐅᔭ
ᑭᕐᓚᖕ�b ᐅᒥᐊᒥ ᐋᒪᓗ ᐊᒍᑎᑦ ᖃᖃᑐᑎᓂᒐᑦ. ᐋᑕᐅᕐᖕ�b
ᑎᑎᑐᖑᓴᒪᐋᒪ ᐅᖃᖑᒍᖑᒪᒪ ᑎᑎᑐᖕᒥ ᓇᓂᕐᓚᖃᑐ ᑕᑦᖃᐅ
ᑎᕐᐊᓗ ᐋᖃᓄᐊᑦ ᐅᒥᐋᓗ ᐅᓂᐊᑐᖕ ᖃᔭᕐᖕᖕ. ᐋᑐᓇᕐᑐᐋᓕᑦ
ᐋᖃᓄᐊᑦ ᐃᑭᑎᕐᓴᓇᐅᑐᑦᑦ ᖃᔭᑐᑐᖕᖕ. ᑕᕐᒪᒪ ᑎᑎᑐᖕᕐᒥ,
ᐃᓴᓇᒍ ᐅᒥᐋᕐᖕb ᒥᑭᑐᐋᐸᒪᔪᖃᓄ ᐅᒪᐋᖃᖃᓄᖃ. ᕐᐊᕐᐊᑐᐋᑦ
ᑕᐋᖃᓄ? ᐋᖃᓄᐋᖃᑎᒪᕐᒥᑦᐅᖕb ᑕᐋᖃᓄ. ᐋᐊᐋᑦ ᐅᐱᑎᕐᖕ�b᷄ᕐᖃ
ᐋᒪᑐᓇ ᐅᒪᐋᕐᖃᓄ ᐋᑐᓄᖃᓄ? ᐋᒪ�b ᐅᐱᐊᑐᐋᖕᓂ. ᐅᔭᕐᐊᑎ
ᔪᒍ ᐋᕐᓇᑐᐋᔪᖃᖃᐅᒪᐃ. ᐅᔭᕐᐊᑎᓄᒍ ᒥᕐᕐᔪᖃᓇᐅᑐᒪ.
ᑐᖕᐱᖃᓇᐅᑐᒍ ᖃᔭᓄᓗ ᐋᒪᓗ ᐋᓇᒥ ᐋᓄᖕᓇ ᓇᕐᓚᖃᓄ
ᐋᕐᓚᒪᑐᖑᑦᐋᕐᖃᒍᓚᖕᑖᑦ ᐋᒪᕐᑐᐋᑦᕐᖃᓗᑕᕐᒥᐅᑎᓄᒪ. ᐋᖃᖃ
ᑕᒍᓚᑦᐋᖑᒪᐋᒪᕐᖃᒍᒪᐋᑐᒍ ᐋᕐᑐᓚᕐᐋᑦ ᐋᕐᑐᐋᓇᖃᑎᕐᖃᒪᖃᕐᒪᐅᑎᓄᒪᑦ. ᐋᒪᓗ
ᖃᒐᔪᑦᑦ ᖃᓄᐅᑎᓇᐅᐸᓇᕐᑐᔪᑦ ᐋᖕᔭᕐᓇ ᖃᑎᕐᖕᑦ ᖃᓄᐅᑎᐅ
ᕐᐋᐅᒪᑦ. ᖃᓄᐅᑎᐅᓇ ᐋᓗᑐᕐᖃᖃᐋᕐᓚᑦᑦ ᐋᖕᔭᐅ ᐋᕐᒥᕐᖃᐅᑐᑦᑦ.

ᐋᑐᐅᕐᒥ ᒥᕐᖕᑐᐋᒪᒪ, ᐋᕐᐋᓇ ᒥᕐᖕᑎᐋᕐᖕᑐᐅᑐᒪ ᑕᐋᒪᒪ.
ᐋᕐᓄᖃᒍ ᐋᖕᕐᐋᓗ ᒥᕐᖕᑐᐋᕐᓄᒪᒪ ᐅᐋᓄᑦ ᐋᖃᐋᖑᐋᕐᖕᑐᐅᑐᒪ.
ᐋᑐᕐᖃᐅᑐᒪᕐᒥ ᐋᖃᐋᕐᖕᑐᐅᑐ.

Happy girls.
Felt pen, ca. 1967

A bird from my mind.
Felt pen, 1968

σ∧ᐊᒉᐊᵇ ᕿ∧ᐊᒉᗽᵇ
ᐃᒪᒉᒍ ᐊᒉᐅᑎᒍᶜ ᑎᑎᗆᒪ,
I967 ᐅᑎᒍᒍ

ᐃᒉᒪᒪᓂ ᕿᐸᒍᐊᵇ
ᐊᒉᐅᑎᒍ ᐃᒪᒉᒍ ᑎᑎᗆᒪ, I968

Three birds.
Felt pen, ca. 1967

ᑯᐸᖕᐊᑦ ᐱᒐᓯᑦ
ᐃᒪᓕᒧ ᐊᓚᐅᑎᒧ ᑎᑎᕋᒐ,
1967 ᐅᑎᓗᒍ

the sewing, my husband would help me. He used to help me with the parkas.

This is how we used to make our clothing. The men would take the skins from the animals and the women would scrape them with the ulus. When I was a young girl and had just married, I did my first sealskin, which was a young, square-flipper seal. I was scraping this seal very quickly and, when it was finished and I stretched it for drying, I saw hundreds of holes! The skin had not been done properly. But I did not do that twice. I tried hard to learn how to sew because I envied the women who could sew nicely. We bought needles from the Bay but we made thread from the whale muscle which was soaked in sea-water and we also used strips of the caribou skin. The clothes could be made out of any kind of skin – caribou, seal or walrus – but I liked the lovely caribou best.

We also had duffel. I do not remember exactly when the duffel came, but I remember having a duffel parka as a

ᑕᐃᒪᓇᑕᒐ ᐊᖑᕆᑎᓂ ᓴᓇᕐᓚᐅᑯᒍᑦ. ᐊᒍᑎᑦ ᐱᓚᐸᓚᐅᑐᑦ ᐅᒪᕗᓂᒃ ᐊᒥᕆᓂᒃ ᐱᔭᓯᑎᒃ ᐊᒪᓗ ᐊᒃᓇᐃᑦ ᑭᔭᑎᕐᓚᐅᑕᕆ ᐅᒃ ᓗᒧ. ᑕᐃᓯᒪᓂ ᓂᕕᐊᔭᐊᒍᓯᒐ ᐅᐃᑕᑲᒥᐅᓯᒐᓗ ᔭᕗᓕᐸᒥ ᓇᔭᐅᑉ ᑭᔭᒐᓂ ᓇᔭᐊᒥᒃ ᑭᔭᑎᓚᐅᔭᒪᕙᒐ ᑕᓯᒥᒐ ᑭᔭᒥᒃ ᐊᒃᓯᐊᓗ ᓯᑲᓯᒐ ᑕᐃᒪ ᐱᔅᑎᖁᑯ ᐃᓂᓚᐅᔭᒪᔅᒐ ᐸᓂᔭᐊᑎᔭ ᓯᒍ, ᑕᑯᓚᐅᔭᒪᕙᒐ ᑭᓚᕈᐊᓗᓂ ᐊᒥᓯᐊᓗᓂᒃ! ᑕᓇ ᑭᔭᒃ ᐱᔭᐊᓂᕆᑕᓗᒐ. ᐃᓚ ᑕᐃᒪᐃᓗᓴᓚᐅᕙᕆᑐᒐ ᑭᒍᓕᒥ. ᐃᓕᓂᐊᔭ ᐊᖁᓯᐊᒪᑎᓕᓚᐅᔭᒪᕙᒐ ᐃᓯᒪᒐᒪ ᐊᒃᓇᒃ ᒥᓯᔭᐊᑐᓴᐅᕙᒃ. ᓂᐅᕕᐸᓯᑕ ᒥᑯᑎᓂᒃ ᓂᐅᕕᕕᒥ ᑭᔭᐊᓂᓕ ᐃᕈᓗᓕᐅᐸᓚᐅᑐᒍᑦ ᑭᓚᓗᒐᐅᑉ ᖑᑭᕆᓂ ᑭᓂᔭᐊᑎᓯᒍ ᑕᑎᐅᒧ ᐃᒪᒧ ᐊᒪᓗᑕᐅᒃ ᐊᑐᐸᓚᐅᒥᕙᒍ ᑐᑐᑉ ᐃᕈᓗᕆᓂ. ᐊᖁᓕᐅᐸᓚᐅᑐᒍ ᑲᖑᑐᐃᓇ ᑭᔭᓂᒃ -- ᑐᑐᔅᓂ ᓇᔭᔅᓂ ᐊᐃᕕᕕᓂᒥᓗᓂ ᐃᓚ ᑐᑐᔅᒥᒃ ᐱᐅᓴᓂᐸᐅᓚᐅᔭᒪᕙᒐ.

ᐊᑎᕆᓴᔅᑲᐸᓚᐅᒥᕙᒍᑕᐅᒃ. ᐊᐅᓚᐳᔅᕆᑐᒐ ᑲᒐ ᐊᑎᕆᓴᔅᒃ ᑎᑭᓂᒪᒐ, ᐃᓚ ᐊᐅᓚᐳᕙᒐ ᐊᑎᕆᑲᓯᒐ ᐊᑎᕆᓴᔅᒥ ᓂᕕᐊᔭᐊ

Overleaf:

ᒪᐱᑐᕋᐅ ᑐᒐᓂᐊ

This is how we played tennis.
Felt pen, 1970

ᐃᒪᓇ ᐸᑕᐸᓚᐅᑐᒍᑦ
ᐃᒪᓕᒧ ᐊᓚᐅᑎᒧᑦ ᑎᑎᑐᒐ, I970

In summer there were always
very big mosquitoes.
Felt pen, 1970

ᐊᐅᔭᒥ ᐊᒋᔪᐊᓗᓂ ᑭᑐᕆᐊᑲᐸᓚᐅᑐᒃ
ᐃᒪᓕᒧ ᐊᓚᐅᑎᒧ ᑎᑎᑐᒐ, I970

little girl. Probably, when the Hudson's Bay post came here, the duffel came along with the company. The duffel was used for the inner parka and for the duffel socks.

ᑯᓗᓯᒐ. ᐃᒪᑲ ᑎᑭᑐᓴᐅᔪᕕᓂ ᓂᐅᕕᑎᑯ ᑎᑭᑎᓗᒋ ᑕᒪᐅᒐ, ᐊᑎᒋᓴᔭ ᑎᑭᑲᑕᐅᑯᑐᕕᓂ ᓂᐅᕕᑎᑯᓄ. ᐊᑎᒋᓴᔭ ᐊᑎᒋᐅᑉ ᐃᓗᐊᓂᑎᓗᒍ ᐊᑐᑕᐅᕙᓚᐅᑐ ᐊᒪᓗ ᐊᓕᑎᓕᐊᕆᓯᒍ.

Each person wore two parkas. Before the duffel came, the first parka, the one nearest the skin, had the fur touching the skin, while the outer parka had the caribou hair outside. When the duffel came, we used it inside. We didn't have money often – we bought the duffel with fox skins.

ᐊᑕᐅᓯ ᐃᓄᒃ ᐊᑎᒋᓂᒃ ᒪᕈᓂᒃ ᐊᑐᐸᓚᐅᑐᒃ. ᐊᑎᒋᓴᔭᒃ ᑎᑭᓚᐅᑎᓇᒍ, ᓯᕗᓕᐸ ᐊᑎᒋ, ᐅᕕᓂᒧ ᑲᓂᓂᐸ ᒥᑯᑲᑎᓗᒍ, ᒥᑯᓕ ᐅᕕᓂᒧ ᐊᑐᐊᑎᓗᒍ, ᓯᓚᐸᒐ ᐊᑎᒋᐅ ᑐᑐᔭᐅᑉ ᒥᑯᒋ ᓯᓚᑕᓂᑎᓗᒋ. ᐊᑎᒋᓴᔭ ᑎᑭᒪ ᐊᑐᓕᓚᐅᑕᕗᑦ ᐃᓗᐊᕆᓯᒍ. ᑭᓇᐅᔭᑲᓚᐅᒋᓇᑕ ᓂᐅᕕᐸᓚᐅᑐᒍ ᐊᑎᒋᓴᔭᒥ ᑎᕆᒐᓂᐊᔭᓄᑦ.

When I made a parka I used to try to make it the way I wanted it to look. I would try to make it look very good. It was not easy and I used to sew on a parka for many days. We always used the finest skin of the young caribou for the head of the parka and, on top, we would put little ears from the baby caribou. It looked very nice. I would also make patterns and designs with different-coloured skins.

ᐊᑎᒋᓕᐅᑐᐊᒐᒪ ᐊᑭᓯᐃᒐᓯᐊᐸᓚᐅᑐᒐ ᑲᓄᐃᑐᑯᔭᓂ. ᐊᑭᓯᐃ ᒐᓯᐊᐸᓚᐅᑐᒐ ᐊᒃᓯᐊᓗ ᐱᐅᔪᓕᐊᕆᒐᓯᓯᒍ. ᐱᑐᐃᓇᕆᐊᑲᓚᐅ ᓯᒪᒋᑐᑦ ᐊᒪᓗ ᒥᓯᐸᓚᐅᑐᒐ ᐊᑎᒋᒥ ᐅᒃᓗᓂ ᐊᒥᓯᓂᒃ. ᑕᐃᒪᒐᓕᒪᓗ ᐊᑐᐸᓚᐅᑐᒍᑦ ᐱᐅᓂᐸᒥ ᑐᑐᐊᒐᒥ ᓇᓴᓕᐊᕆᓯᒍ ᐊᑎᒋᒧᑦ ᐊᒪᓗ ᑲᒐᓄᓯᓯᒐ ᑐᑐᔭᐱᐅᑉ ᓯᐅᑎᑯᓗᒋᓂᒃ. ᐱᐅᔪᐸᓗᕙᓚᐅᑐᑦ. ᐅᒃᑐᑎᓕᐅᐸᓚᐅᒥᔪᒍᑦ ᐊᑭᓯᓯᒪᓂᒋᓂᓗ ᐊᔭᒋᒋᑐᓂ ᑕᒃᓴᑲᑎᓗᒋ ᑐᑐᔭᐃᑦ.

Before we started living in one place, as we do now, we used to walk very long distances and the boots would wear

ᐊᑕᐅᓯᓴᐃᓇᒥᒋᓇᓯᑕ ᓄᓇᒥ ᑕᐃᒪᓇᐃᓕᒐᑕ ᒪᓇ ᐱᓯᐸᓚᐅᑐᒍ ᐅᒐᓯᑐᐊᓗᒧ ᑲᒥᕗᓗ ᓯᑯᓴᐅᑎᒋᐊᐱᐸᓯᑎ. ᐱᔭᕆᓚᐅᓯᒪᕙᓚᐅ

On top of the parka we put
little ears from the baby caribou.
Felt pen, 1970

ᑐᑐᔮᐱᐅᑉ ᓱᐅᑎᑭᓂ ᐊᑎᑭᐅᑉ ᓇᔅᒐᖁ
ᓱᕙᓚᐅᑐᒍᑦ ᐃᒪᓕᓗᑦ ᐊᓚᐅᑎᓗᑦ
ᑎᑎᑐᒐ, 1970

Engraving, 1962

ᐅᑯᓱᔅᔭᒥ ᔅᓇᒍᐊᒐᒃ, 1962

out quickly. I was never finished with making mukluks. I also would make new soles and sew them on the worn boots. For boots we used only sealskin and, once the skin was cleaned, we would chew it so that the mukluks would be soft. It was hard to do but it worked well.

I also made 'qutugut', which were worn above the boots and covered the legs. This is how it used to be with qutugut – there was string with a knot on the end, which went up and hooked over the pants above.

When James Houston, whom we call Sowmik – the left-handed one – came to Cape Dorset and told me to draw the old ways, I began to put the old costumes into the drawings and prints. Some days I am really tired of the old ways – so much drawing. But many liked my parkas – many people really used to like my clothes.

I am too old now to make any more and my eyes are not good. But every year I still make sealskin pants for Kaka.

ᕙᑭᑐᒐ ᑲᒥᓕᐅᓯᒐ. ᖁᑕᓂᓗ ᐊᓕᔨᕙᓯᒐ ᑲᒥᑦ ᐊᓕᓱᒪᓂᑭᓂ ᒥᓯᐸᓯᑭ. ᑲᒥᑲᐸᓚᐅᑐᒍ ᓇᓱᒐᕕᓂᓂ ᑭᓱᐊᓂ ᑕᐃᒪ ᑭᓱᑦ ᓴᓗᒪᓴᑎᑐᐊᒐᑎᒍ ᑭᓂᑎᐸᓚᐅᑕᕗᑦ ᑲᒥᑦ ᑭᑐᑐᓂᐊᒪᑕ. ᐃᓱᐊᑭᑐᐊᓗᕙᓚᐅᕙᕙ ᐃᓚ ᐱᒍᓇᓱᐊᐸᓚᐅᕙᕙ.

ᑯᑐᒍᑦᓕᐅᐸᓚᐅᒥᕙᒐ ᑲᒥᑦ ᑯᓚᒐᓂᑎᓗᒍ ᐊᑐᑕᐅᕙᓚᐅᑐᒥᒃ ᓂᐅᑭᔭᑎᑯᑎᓂᒃ. ᑕᐃᒪᓇᑕᒐ ᑕᐃᒪᐃᑐᕙᓚᐅᓱᒪᕙᑦ ᑯᑐᒍᑦᖁ ᐊᒃᓯᓇᑲᓗᑎ ᑭᓚᓱᒪᓗᑎᒃ ᐃᓯᒥᒍᑦ, ᑕᐸᐅᒐᒐᕙᒥ ᑭᓚᓱᒪᓗᓂ ᑲᓕᑦ ᑯᓚᒐᒍᑦ.

ᑕᐃᓯᒪᓂ ᔮᐃᒥᓱ ᕙᓯᑕᓐ ᓴᐅᒥᐅᓂᕋᑕᐅᕙ, ᑭᒐᖁᒪ ᑕᐃᒪ ᐅᑲᐅᑎᓚᐅᓱᒪᔮᒐ ᑎᑎᑐᔮᑯᓯᓂᒐ ᐅᕙᓱᐊᕈᓂᑕᓂ ᐃᓕᓱᕙᓕᓚᐅᑐᒐ ᑎᑎᑐᔮᑐᖁᑦ ᐱᐅᓱᑐᑲᕕᓂᓂ ᑎᑎᑐᔮᓱᒪᕙᖁᓯᑭ ᐊᒪᓗ ᐊᔨᓚᐅᓱᒪᕙᖁ. ᐃᓚᓂ ᐊᒃᓯᐊᓗ ᑕᑲᓱᒪᕙᓗᒐ ᐅᕙᓱᐊᕈᓂᑕᓂ ᐊᒃᓯᐊᓗ ᑎᑎᑐᔮᑎᐊᔅ. ᐃᓚ ᐊᒥᓯᖁ ᐱᐅᑭᔮᐅᕙ ᐊᑎᑭᑲ ᐊᒥᓯᖁ ᐃᖁᖁᑦ ᐊᒃᓯᐊᓗ ᐱᐅᑭᔮᐅᕙᓚᐅᕙᕙ ᐊᖁᕋᑲ.

ᒪᓇᓕ ᓂᑭᐅᒍᒪ ᓴᓇᓚᐅᓱᒪᒍᓂᑐᒐ ᐃᔨᑲᓗ ᐱᐅᓱᐊᒍᓂᒪᑕ. ᐃᓚ ᓯᓕ ᐊᖃᒍᑕᒪ ᑲᓕᓕᐅᐸᑐᒐ ᓇᓱᔮᓂ ᑲᑲᐅᑉ ᑲᓕᔅᑭᓂ. ᐊᑕᑕᒥᑎᑐᑦ, ᑲᑲ ᖁᓇᑲᑎᑲᒍᒪᔮᑭᑐᑦ ᐃᖁᑲᑎᒥᓂᒃ ᐊᒪᓗ

Bearded seals around ice.
Felt pen, ca. 1967

ᐅᔪᐃᑦ ᓯᑯᒥᑐᑦ
ᐃᒪᓕᒧ ᐊᓚᐅᑎᒧ ᑎᑎᑐᒐ,
I967 ᐅᑎᓗᒍ

Travelling by dog team (detail).
Coloured pencil and felt pen,
ca. 1967

ᑭᒧᓯᑐᑦ (ᐃᒪᐃᓕᒐᓂᒐ)
ᑕᒃᓴᓕᓄ ᐊᓚᐅᑎᓄ ᐊᒪᓗ ᐃᒪᓕᒧᑦ
ᑎᑎᑐᒐ, I967 ᐅᑎᓗᒍ

Like his father, Kaka does not want to live with other people and he stays in camp. Like his father, Kaka is a very good hunter and every year he gets the most beautiful skins from a special seal – the 'kasigiak'. The skins are lovely and dark, and he brings them to me and I must make these pants.

I liked the old clothes but I like the new clothes, too.

In the old days men were very good hunters. They had to keep busy to feed the dogs and the family. We depended on the dogs and Ashoona always had a very good team. Dogs would have puppies and there were always from five to ten. They never had to be trained, they knew by instinct. They were clever and dangerous, too, but when they were full and happy, they went fast. Sometimes in the camps in a bad winter, the dogs used to starve, but Ashoona always brought lots of food. Some days he would bring ten seals from one day's hunting. He would cut meat for the dogs even in winter.

ᐃᒃᓗᑲᕆᑐᒥᑲᑕᑐᒃ. ᐊᑕᑕᒥᑎᑐ ᑲᑲ ᐊᒍᓇᓯᐊᓯᑎᐸᓗ ᐊᒪᓗ ᐊᕋᒍᑕᒪ ᐱᐅᔪᐸᓗᓂ ᓇᓯᐸᑐ ᒥᑯᓯᐊᑭᑐᐸᓗᓂ ᓇᓯᓂ -- ᑲᓯᒋᐊᓂ. ᑕᑯᐊ ᒥᑯᕆᑦ ᐱᐅᔪᐸᐃᓗᑦ ᑭᓂᓗᑎᓗ ᐊᒪᓗ ᑲᐃ ᓯᐸᓗᓂ ᑭᓯᓂᒃ ᑲᓚᓚᐊᓴᑲᓂᒃ.

ᐱᐅᓴᐸᓚᐅᑐᒐ ᐅᕆᓯᐊᕈᓂᑕᓂ ᐊᓄᕋᓂ, ᐃᓚ ᐱᐅᓴᒥᔪᒐᑕᐅᒃ ᓄᑕᓂ ᐊᓄᕋᓂ. ᐅᕆᓯᐊᕈ ᐊᒍᑎᑦ ᐊᒍᓇᓯᐊᓯᑎᐅᕆᓚᐅᔪᔪ. ᓄᑲᓚᐅᓯᒪᕆᓯᑎᒃ ᓂᑎᑲᐃᓯᑎᒃ ᑭᒥᓂ ᐃᓚᒥᓂᓗ. ᑭᒥᓂᒃ ᐃᑲᔪᑎᑲᓚᐅᑐ ᐊᒪᓗ ᐊᒃᓯᐊᓇ ᑌᒪᒐᓗ ᐱᐅᔪᓂ ᑭᒥᑲᐸᓗᓂ. ᑭᒥᑦ ᑭᒥᐊᕋᑕᐸᓗᑎ ᐊᒪᓗ ᑕᐃᒪᒐ ᑭᒥ 5-ᒍᓗᑎ IO-ᒍᓗ ᑎᓗᓂ. ᐃᓕᓴᑎᐊᑲᐸᓚᐅᕆᑐ, ᑲᐅᔨᒪᔪᐃ ᐊᐅᓚᓂᑐᐃᓇᒧ. ᐊᑭᑐᓯᓚᒐᒥ ᑯᕕᐊᓯᓚᒐᒥᓗ ᓯᑲᑐᕆᓚᐅᑐ. ᐃᓚᓂᑯ ᓄᓇᑎᓂ ᓯᓚ ᐱᐅᑎᓇᒍ ᑭᒥ ᑲᐸᓚᐅᑐ ᐃᓚ ᐊᒃᓯᐊᓇ ᑕᐃᒪᒐ ᑎᑭᐅᔨᕆ ᓚᐅᑐ ᓂᑭᐊᓗᓂ -- ᐃᓚᓂ IO-ᓂ ᓇᓯᓂ ᐊᓇᕋᐅᔨᕆᓚᐅᑐᒃ ᐅᒃᓗᒥ ᐊᑕᐅᓯᒥ ᐊᒍᓇᓯᐊᓯᓂ. ᓇᓯᓂ ᐱᓚᐸᓚᐅᑐ ᑭᒥᓄᕋᓴ ᒥᓂᒃ ᐅᑭᐅᒐᓴᒥ.

There seemed to be more animals in the old days. There were more whales and more seals and, just quite recently, there were lots of narwhales around Cape Dorset. But today the animals don't seem to come into the settlements much. Now they have all these motors and the animals hear them and run away. Now there are motors everywhere, but dogs were safer than skidoos. Skidoos can break down out there, far from Cape Dorset; and dogs will bark when they see a polar bear.

In the old days, when men left the camp, they would always give the women something that killed – a gun. But I used to be very poor at shooting and I remember one day, although we had lots of food, I wasted a whole box of ammunition trying to kill a little seal. I knew it would get away. But though I have never shot a caribou, there are very few birds that I have not caught.

When I was a little girl my father and mother taught me how to catch a goose. Four people would corner a goose

ᐅᕙᖏᐊᐳᓐᓗᒍ ᐅᒪᔭᖃᐅᓕᐅ�᙮ᐸᕚᐅᑐᔭᖅ᙮ ᑭᓴᓗᖃ᙮ᐅᕐᓴ ᐊᒪᓗ ᐊᕿᖃᐅᕚᕐᓂ ᒪᖏᑦ ᑭᕐᐊᓂ ᐊᖓᓐᑕᖃᑊᒥ ᐊᕐᕕᓂ ᑭᑕ ᖃ᙮ᐊᓂ᙮ ᐃᓓ ᒪᖓ ᐅᒪᔭᐊ ᑎᑭᕐᐊᐅᐅᕐᓚᔭᖖᒪᐃᑦ ᓄᐊᓚᓄ᙮ ᒪᓓ᙮ ᐊᕐᕕᓂ ᐊᐅᓚᐅᑎᖃᓓᓚᑦ ᐅᒪᔭᓄ ᑐᖕᖅᐅᕕᖅ ᓓᑦ ᑭᓕᖅᕿᖅᐅᓐᓗᓓᑦ᙮ ᒪᓓᖖ ᐊᐅᓚᐅᑎᖃᓓᓚᑦ ᐊᕐᒥᓕᖅ᙮ ᐃᓓ ᑭᒥ ᐊᕿᐊᖏᔭ᙮ ᕐᖅᑐᓂ᙮ ᕐᖅᑐ ᑲᒍᓐᑐᕚ ᕐᒍᔭᖖᓂ ᐊᕐᒥᐊᒥᖅ᙮ ᑭᓕᐊᑦ ᐅᓕᕐᑕᓐᓗᓂ᙮ ᐊᒪᓗ ᑭᒥ᙮ ᒍᒍᕐᖖᐅᒍ ᑕᑊᓓᐊᒥᖅ ᓄᓂᖅᖅ᙮

ᐅᕙᖏᐊᐳᓐᓗᒍ ᑕᐊᕐᓚᖖᓂ ᐊᒍᖖᑊ ᑭᓚᐊᓚᖅᐸᖏᖅᓂ ᑕᐊᓐᓗ ᐊᖅᖖᐊᑦ ᑐᑭᕐᒍᑐᖅᖖᓗᖖᓂ ᑐᖖᕐᐸᓚᑐᖖ – – ᑯᑭᐅᑎᖅ᙮ ᐃᓓ ᕐᕐᐊᒍᖖᐊᖖᑭᐊᐅᑐᑐᒪ ᐊᒪᓗ ᐊᐅᓚᖅᖖᐊᒪᖖ ᐊᑭᐅᑊᖖᐊᕐᒪᖅ᙮ ᓂᕿᖖᐊ ᓗᖖᐊᐅᑦ᙮ ᐊᕿᖖᑯᐅᑐᖅᖖᐊᒪᖖ ᐃᓗᐊᐅᑐᖕᖅᖖ ᐊᕿᐊᖅᒥ ᓇᑯᑐᐊᖕᖅᒥ ᐊᓂᐅᑐᓗᖕᖅ ᑐᑭᕐᒍᐊᕐᐊᖅᒥ᙮ ᑲᐅᕐᒪᕐᒪᖖ ᕐᖖᑊᒥᕐᕐᐊᖖᒪᖅ᙮ ᐃᓓ ᕐᕐᐊᖖᓚᕐᓚᖕᖅᖖᑐᐊᐅᑐᖖᒪ ᐅᑐᖖᒥᖖ᙮ ᐊᕿᖅᔭᓗᖖᑊᖕᖖ ᖕᐊᖖᐅᐊᖖᖖ ᖕᐊᖖᐊᖕᐅᑭᖕᑯ ᖕᖖᐊᖖ ᐊᓄᓂᓓᓂ᙮

ᑕᐊᕐᓚᖖᓂ ᓂᐃᐊᕐᐊᖖᓗᖖᑊᖅᓂᐅᑦ ᐊᑦᑭᖕᓂ ᖕᐊᖕᐊᓗ ᐊᑭᖕᑐᖕᐊᖕᐅᑊ ᒪᐊᑦ ᖖᐊ ᑭᑎᕐᕐᒍᒪᑊᑊᒪᖖ ᖕᐊᕐᒥ᙮ ᕐᒪᑭ ᐃᖖᐊ ᕐᐅᖕᑊᕐᐅᑊᒏ

My parents taught me how to catch a goose (Pitseolak, lower left; her father, top left; her mother, top right; and a woman from the camp).
Felt pen, 1970

ᐊᓇᓇᒐᓄᑦ ᐊᑕᑕᒐᓄᓗ ᓂᓕᒋᐅᓴᑎᑕᐅᓚ ᐅᐳᒐ (ᐱᓯᐅᓚ, ᐱᓯᐅᓚᑉ ᐊᑕᑕᒐ, ᐊᓇᓇᒐ, ᐊᒪᓗ ᐊᒃᓇᒃ ᓄᓇᑲᑎᒐ ᑭᒍ ᓕᐸᒃ.) ᐃᒪᓕᒧᑦ ᐊᓚᐅᑎᒧᑦ ᑎᑎᑐᒐ
I970

Man trying to catch a goose.
Stone cut, 1964

ᐊᒍᑎᑦ ᓂᒃᓕᓂᐊᑐᑦ
ᐅᔭᕋᒥ ᑎᑎᑐᒐ, I964

and then my parents would tell me to run up behind it, hooting and shouting, and put my foot on its neck. I'd run and I'd catch the goose and I'd stand there waving my arms like a bird. Sometimes we'd all have headaches from shouting and yelling.

In 'isha', the season when the geese lose their feathers, they are very easy to catch. They can't fly then and you can catch them easily on the grass. Just before I was born they used to drive the moulting geese into stone pens, but we didn't bother with pens. Geese are best found in mossy areas. Their feet are very sensitive and they won't go on the rocks. They always go where it's mossy or where there's grass.

Sometimes an Eskimo man will take a long rope with a loop on the end and place the loop on the ground. Then the Eskimo man will hide behind a rock and, when a goose passes over the loop, he'll pull the rope and he catches the goose.

ᓂᓕᒐᓯᐸᓚᐅᑐ ᑕᐃᒪ ᐊᑕᑕᑯᓄ ᐅᑲᐅᑎᔭᐅᕙᓚᐅᑐᒐ ᐅᓚᑯᔭᐅ ᓯᒐ ᐅᒐᑕᓄ, ᓂᐱᑯᑐᓗᒐ ᑲᐃᒐᓕᓗᒐᓗ ᑐᓕᓗᒍ ᑯᒋᓯᒐᒍᑦ ᐅᓚᐸᓚᐅᑐᒐ ᓂᓕᒥᒃ ᑎᒍᓯᓚᒐᓯᒐ ᐃᓚᒐᓂᓗ ᓇᒋᑐᐃᓇᐸᓯᒐ ᓴᕙᓯᒐ. ᐃᓚ ᓂᓕᓚᐅᓯᒪᕙᒐ. ᐃᓚᓂᑯᑦ ᓂᐊᑯᒍᐸᓚᐅᑐᒐ ᓂᐱᑯᑐᕕᓂᐅᒧ ᑲᐃᒐᓕᑐᕕᓂᐅᒧᓗ.

ᐃᓴᐅᑎᓗᒋ ᓂᓕᑦ ᐃᓴᕈᐃᔭᓯᒪᑎᓗᒋ, ᑎᒍᓴᐅᑎᒋᒍᓇᑐᐊᐱᑦ. ᑎᒥᒍᓇᔭᒋᒪᑕ ᑕᐃᒪ ᑎᒍᔭᐅᓴᐅᑎᒋᒍᓇᑐ ᓄᓇᕋᔭᒥ. ᐃᓄᓕᒋ ᓗᐊᕋᐱᑎᓗᒍ ᐃᓄᐃᑦ ᐃᓴᓂ ᐅᔭᕋᐅ ᐃᓗᐊᓄᓯᑲᑕᑐᕕᓂ ᐃᓚ ᑲᒪᕙᓚᐅᔭᒋᑐᒐ ᐃᓗᐊᓄᕕᓂᒃ. ᓂᓚᓂ ᑕᑯᓴᐅᑎᒋᒍᐊᓇᑐᒃ ᓄᓇᔭᓕᒥ. ᐃᓯᒐᒋ ᑕᓯᒍᐊᑐᐸᓗᐃ ᐊᒪᓗ ᐅᔭᕋᔭᑯᓂᐅᔭᒐᑎ. ᑕᐃᒪ ᓄᓇᒐᔭᓕᒧᔅ ᐅᕙᓗᓂ ᓄᓇᑐᐃᓇᓚᒧ.

ᐃᓚᓂᑯ ᐃᓄᒃ ᐊᒍᑎᒃ ᐊᒃᓯᓇᒥ ᑎᒍᓯᕙᓚᐅᑐᒃ ᑕᑭᔦᑎᓗᒍ ᐊᒃᓯᓇ ᓯᓗᑲᑎᓗᒍ ᑕᐃᒪ ᓯᓗᒐ ᓄᓇᒧᓯᒍ. ᑕᐃᒪ ᑕᑎᓯᒪᓚ ᒐᓯᓂ ᐅᔭᕋᐅᑉ ᐊᒐᑕᓂ ᑕᐃᒪ ᓂᓕᒃ ᓯᓗᒐᑕ ᓇᓚᒍᓕᑐᐊᒪᑦ ᐊᒃᓯᓇᒥ ᓄᓯᐃᓚᒐᓯᓂ ᑕᐃᒪᒃ ᓂᒃᓕᐸᓚᐅᑐᑦ.

Flower spirit.
Engraving, 1968

ᐱᑐᕐᑫᖅ
ᐅᑯᕐᖅᕝᒥ ᑎᑎᑐᒐ, I968

It's fun to chase a goose and it's always fun to be around animals – they are meat.

I can't remember the first time I tasted the white man's food, but I do remember one incident. At the time, they were building the Hudson's Bay post's big warehouse and I was just a little girl. I remember watching people unload the supply boat, and I was crying very hard. They gave me a pilot biscuit and I really liked it.

I like the white man's food but I think the old food was better for Eskimos. In the old days we had more food from animals and we didn't get sick so much. We ate the food raw. We used to eat seal, whale, caribou, ducks and ptarmigan all raw, though we used to cook the goose, and goose cooked is very good. We also used to cook the polar bear, though some people ate it raw.

We had fruit in the summer. We used to pick the berries on the tundra, and something else we ate was dulse. We

ᑯᐱᐊᓇᑐ ᐅᑌᖃᑎᐊᕐ ᓄᓪᒃᑫᖅᑉ ᐊᒪᓗ ᑕᐅᒪ ᑯᐱᐊᓇᓱᓂ ᐅᒪᕐᓪᒥᕐᐊᒥ -- ᐅᒪᕈᐊᑦ ᓂᕐᐅᑉᒪᒥᑭ.

ᐊᑉᓚᕐᕐᐅᑐ ᑯᒪ ᕐᐳᑖᐸᒥ ᑲᓴᓇ ᓂᕐᖠᓂ ᐅᑐᓂᒪᒪᒪ ᐃᓐ ᐊᑉᓚᕐᐊᕐᒪᐊ ᐊᐸᐅᕐᒥ ᐅᑐᕐᒪᒪ. ᑕᐊᕐᒪᓗᐅᑌᐅᑐᓱᒍ ᐊᖅᓱᑲᐅᑐᕐ ᕐᒪᕐᐊ ᓂᐅᐱᐊᑐ ᐅᕐᑐᐊᓇᑳᑐᐊᒍᓗᓂ ᐊᒪᓗ ᑕᐊᕐᒪᓂ ᓂᕐᐊᐊ ᕐᐊᑯᓗᓄᐊᓇᐅᕐᐅᑐᕐᒪᕐᐊᒪ. ᐊᑉᓚᕐᐊᕐᒪᒪ ᑖᑯᓄᐅᒪᕐᒍᒪ ᐃᓄᓂᒃ ᐅᕐᕐᐊᐅᓄ ᐅᕐᐊᐱ ᐅᕐᕐᒥᓂ ᐊᒪᓗ ᕐᑲᓚᑐᕐᒪᕐᐊᒪ ᐊᖅᕐᐊᓱ. ᐊᐊᑐ ᑕᐅᑲᓚᑐᕐᒪᕐᐊᒪ ᕐᐸᓚᑐᒥ (ᖃᑯᕐᒥ) ᕐᑎᕐᒥᑭ ᐱᐅᕐᓚᐅ ᕐᒪᕐᐅᕐ ᐊᖅᕐᐊᓱᑭ.

ᑲᓱᐊᑦ ᓂᕐᐅᕐᒥᓂᕐ ᐱᐅᖅᓱᑐᒪ ᐃᓐ ᐅᕐᕐᐊᑐᓂᑕᑲᑭ ᓂᕐᒪᓂᑭ ᐱᐅᓂᖅᐅᕐᐅᑌᕐᕐᒪᑐᒪ ᐃᓄᐅᑦ. ᐅᕐᕐᐊᑐᓂᑕᑐᒍ ᓂᕐᖃᓂᖅᐅᕐ ᑐᐅᑯᒍ ᐅᒪᕐᐊᓂᓂ, ᑲᓱᒪᕐᐊᑲᐅᑐᕐᒪᕐᓱᑲᑕ. ᓂᑭᓚᑐᒍ ᖃᒪᕐᑐᒥ ᓂᕐᖃᒥ. ᓂᑭᓚᑐᒍ ᖃᒥᕐ ᐸᑲᓚᒥᕐ, ᑐᑐᐊᓄᒥᕐ, ᓂᑎᐊᓂ ᐊᖃᕐᒥᓄᐅ ᐃᓄᖃᑎ ᑲᑲᕐᒪᑎᓇᒥᕐ ᐊᒪᕐᑲᐅᑐᕐᓚᐊᑐᒍᐊ ᓄᑐᒥᕐ, ᐊᒪᓗ ᓄᑭ ᐊᒪᕐᑲᒪᓂᕐ ᐱᐅᑲᑯᓗ. ᐊᒪᕐᑲᑐᒥᕐᐊᒍᑦ ᓄᒪᐱᓂᕐᒃ, ᐃᓄᐃᑦ ᐃᓂᕐᒥ ᒥᕐᖃᑲᑐᕐᓱᐊᕐᒥᒪ.

Eskimo camp scene.
Engraving, 1967

ᑐᐱᐅᑦ
ᐅᑯᕈᖕᒃᖢᕐ ᑎᑎᑐᒪ, I967

used to hunt for dulse around the beaches. Sometimes, when the men went hunting, they would bring back dulse for the women. Eskimo people believe that it has some medicine in it; when they are sick they feel better if they have some.

Sometimes in the winter it was boring in the igloo but we never stayed inside much. We had warmer clothes in those days and it used to be fun when It was windy. The fathers would make toy sleds for their sons and daughters to slide on and, when the children had their sleds and their toy whips, they would play outside most of the day. Now they are in school all day and they have the habit of staying indoors.

Very often in those days when we felt happy in camp, Ashoona and I would play the accordion. My favourite brother once gave me an accordion and we both could play. The little children would come and dance. Kaka used to dance a lot.

ᐸᐅᒪᒃᐸᑕᐅᑎᓲ ᐊᐅᖤᒍ. ᐸᐅᒪᑦᑕᑕᐅᕋᕈ ᓄᒥ, ᐊᒪᔾ
ᐊᕐᓂ ᓂᑎᐸᑕᐅᒥᖢᒍᑦ ᑭᑯᓂ. ᑭᑯᐊᔪᐅᑕᐅᑐᒍ ᓯᖅᒥ.
ᐃᓂ, ᐊᒍᑎᑦ ᐊᒍᓇᔾᐊᖏ ᐊᓇᖥᐊᑕᐅᔾᔪ ᑭᑯᐊᖕ
ᐊᖃᐊ ᓂᑎᒪᖢᒐᓂ. ᐃᓄᐃ ᐊᓄᐊᔾᐅᑎᖃᑐᖕᕈᒥ ᑭᑯᐊᒥ;
ᖃᓄᒪᓈᑐᐊᒪ ᐊᑭᖦᑕᐅᔾᔾ ᓂᑎᐅᐊᒥ ᑭᑯᐊᒥ.

ᐃᓂ ᐅᑭᐅᒪ ᐊᑭᔪᓇᖅᑕᐅᑐ ᐊᖕ ᔪᐊᒪᒥ ᐃᒐ ᐃᓇᔾᓂᕋᖝ
ᐅᖥᕐᑐᔾᒃ. ᐅᑯᓂᖥᖕᖃᖕ ᐊᓄᖅᖃᖜᐊᑐᖖᑕ ᑕᐊᕈᒪᓂ ᐊᒪᔾ
ᔪᐊᔪᐊᖥᐊᑐ ᐊᔪᓂᐸᖢᐊᒪ. ᐊᑕᖢᔾᐊᑦ ᐱᒍᔾᐊᖥᐊᖤᐊᑐᖤ
ᖃᔾᓄᒍᔾᐊᖥᐊᔾᓂ ᐊᖃᓂᒪ ᐸᓂᕈᓇ ᕐᔾᖃᐅᖥᓂᓇ ᐱᐊᖥᐊ
ᖃᔾᓄᖃᖢᒥᖤ ᐃᐃᖃᐅᑐᔾᐊᔾᓇ, ᐱᔾᐊᖤᖃᖢᐊᑐᖤ ᕐᒥ
ᐅᖤ ᔾᖤᖢᖃᖥ. ᒪᓇ ᐃᓂᓇᐊᖤᒥ ᐊᖤ ᓇᖤᔾᐅᒪᐃᓇᔾᔾᐊᖤᖤ.

ᔾᖣᐊᔾᖃᖕᑕ ᓄᓇᓂᖤ ᐊᖤᐊᖤᓄ ᓂᖅᓄᑎᔾᐊᑕᐅᔾᔾ ᑕᔾᖃᐊᒥ.
ᐊᖓᓇᖥᖝᑦ ᐊᐊᔾᑐᑕᐅᔾᑕᐅᖥᒪᖥᒪ ᑕᔾᖃᐊᒥ ᖤᖥᐅᑎᒥ ᑕᒪᖤᖥ
ᓂᖥᐅᑎᔾᐊᖤᔾᓄᔾ. ᐱᔾᓕᖤᔾᐊᐃᖤ ᖃᐃᖥᐊᑕᐅᔾᔾ ᑕᖤᖥᑎᐊᔾᖤᖕᖝ.
ᖃᖃ ᑕᖤᖥᖥᐢᖦᐱᐊᔾᓄᖥᐊᑕᐅᔾᔾᖝ.

Ashoona used to like to juggle. He could keep three
small stones in the air and sometimes, just for two seconds,
I could keep three stones up there, too.

We played lots of games. One game was 'illupik' – jumping
over the 'avatuk', the sealskin float that hunters used to
tie to the harpoons so the seals would stay on the water
after they were killed. I hear young people in Cape Dorset
still try to jump the avatuk at the youth club meetings.

Another game was the Eskimo tennis! This is how we
played this game – we threw a ball underhand and tried to
catch it in a sealskin racket. The racket was called an
'autuk'. We made the ball from caribou skin and stuffed it
with something. We used to play this game a lot, even
in winter. It was a good game, but they don't play it now;
they are following the world.

It was always most joyful when people came together
in Cape Dorset. Every year we would make three trips to

ᐊᖅᕈᓇ ᐊᖕ ᓄᑭᑎᓈᖅ ᐱᐅᖅᓴᑳᐅᕐᖅ. ᐱᒪᕐᓂᖅ ᐅᖅᖑᓯᓂ
ᑲᑕᑎᒍᓇᐸᑳᐅᑐᖅ ᐊᓓᓄ ᒪᕈᐱᑲᐱᓐᕐ ᐱᒪᕐᓄᑕᖅ
ᐊᖕ ᓄᑭᑐᒍᓇᒻᕈᒪ.

ᐊᒻᕐᐊᔪᓂ ᐱᔪᐊᕐᖅᖃᐸᑳᐅᑐ. ᐊᑕᐅᕐ ᐱᔪᐊᕐᕆ ᐃᓄᐱ ‐‐
ᐊᐸᑕᐅᑦ ᑲᐅᓄᑦ ᒥᕐᑕᕐᓂ, ᐊᐸᑕᒥᖅ ᐊᔪᓇᕐᐊᑎ ᐳᐊᕐᕿᑲ
ᐅᕈ ᑭᓕᒍᓪᕈᒍ ᐅᐊᓕᒍᑕ ᑕᐊᒪ ᓇᖅᖅ ᑭᐱᓇᐊᕐᒪ ᓄᑲᑕᕐᕆ
ᓚᖃᓂ. ᔪᖅᖅᐊᑐᒪ ᐅᐱᖅᐊᐃᑦ ᑭᓚᓂ ᕈᐊᕐᕿ ᒥᕐᑎᑐᕐᑎᓂᕐᒍ
ᐊᐸᑕᒍᐊᑦ ᐅᐱᖅᐊᐃᓚ ᑲᑎᓚᑎᓄᒍᕐ. ᐊᕈᒪᑕᐅᕐ ᐱᔪᐊᕐᕈᕐ ᐊᖕᐃ
ᐊᕐᕐᒪᓚ: ᐃᓚᓇᑕᒪ ᐱᔪᐊᕝᑲᐅᑐᒍᑦ ᑕᕐᒪᒪ ᐱᔪᐊᕐᕆᒍᕐ ‐‐
ᐊᕐᕿᑕᕈ ᐊᖕᕐ ᐊᓕᐅᑦ ᐊᑕᒍ ᐊᑐᓪᒍᕐᕿᑕᕈ ᓇᕐᐅᑦ
ᑭᕐᒪ ᐊᖕᕐ. ᑕᓇ ᐊᖕᕐ ᑕᐃᓕᖅᐳᑕᐅᑐ ᐊᐅᑕᕐ. ᐊᖕ ᓱᑕᐅ
ᐸᑕᐅᕐᑐᑦ ᐊᐅᑕᑕᖅᐸᑕᐅᕐᑐᒍ ᔪᑦ ᑭᒪᓚᓂ ᐊᓱᐊᒍᓚ ᐱᑕᕐ
ᔪᕐᒍ ᑭᕐᒍᑐᐊᒥᕐᖅ. ᑕᓇ ᐱᒍᐊᕐᓇᐸᑕᐅᕐᕐᔪᕐ ᑕᐊᒪᒪᓪᖅ,
ᐅᕐᑭᒪᕐᕆ ᐱᒍᐊᒍᕐᐸᑕᐅᕐ ᐊᓓ ᒪ ᐱᒍᐊᑎᕐᕐᒍᒍᐊᒪᓪ,
ᒪᓚᒍᕐᕿᖅ ᕈᕐᐊᒍᕐᖅ.

ᑕᐊᒪᒪᒍᒪ ᔪᐊᔪᐊᕐᑕᐅᑐᕐᕐᔪᖅ ᐊᖕᐃᑦ ᑎᑭᐅᑭᓚᒪ ᑭᓚᕐᖅ.
ᐊᕈᒍᑕᒪ ᐱᒪᕐᓈᕐᑦ ᐊᐅᑕᓚᓚᑕᐅᑐᒍ ᑭᒪᕐᐊᕐᑦ ᑭᒍᕐᕿᑦ.

One game we played was 'illupik' – jumping over the sealskin float.
Felt pen, 1970

ᐱᒍᐊᐸᓚᐅᑕᑕ ᐃᓚᒐ ᐃᓗᐱᒃ ᒥᓯᑲᑕᓯ
ᑕ ᐊᕿᑕᒧ ᐃᒪᓕᒧᑦ ᐊᓚᐅᑎᒧ ᑎᑎᑐᒐ
1970

Cape Dorset with the dog team. When the nights were light we would travel after midnight and build an igloo when we stopped. It used to be cold when it was windy! We would go to Dorset to sell the fox skins to the Bay and get supplies. We got good prices for the fox then; fox used to be worth a lot. We would buy in exchange what we call the grub – the white man's food – tea, flour, salt, baking powder and shortening.

We always made one trip in summer to see the Nascopie. This ship used to bring all the supplies for the year to the Bay. We were always happy to see the Nascopie. One year the Nascopie went on some rocks coming into Dorset and was wrecked. Many people got things from the wreckage. I remember my son, Kiawat, got a primus stove and some blankets. He saw other people getting things and decided he should have something, too.

In those days, a lot of people and families would spend a long summer in Cape Dorset and then, before the weather

ᐅᓄᐊᒥ ᑕᑐᒍᓇᐃᑐᐊᒪᑦ ᐊᐅᓚᐸᓚᐅᑐᒍ ᑭᑎᕋᒋᓯᒪᓕᑎᓗᒍ
ᐅᓄᐊᒐ ᐃᓗᕕᒐᓕᐅᐸᓯᑕ ᓄᑲᑲᑕ. ᑭᐅᓇᐸᓚᐅᔪᔪ ᐊᓄᑎᓕᒪ!
ᑭᒐᓕᐊᐸᓚᐅᑐᒍ ᓂᐅᕗᑎᑲᒋᐊᑐᓯᑕ ᑎᑎᒐᓂᐊᔭᓂ ᓂᐅᕕᑎᑯᓄᑦ
ᓂᐅᕕᑎᐊᑐᓯᑕᓗ ᓂᐅᕕᐊᓴᒥᒃ. ᐊᑭᑲᓯᐊᑲᑯᔭᐅᕿᓚᐅᕋᑕ
ᑎᑎᒐᓂᐊᔭᓂᒃ ᑕᐃᓯᒪᓂ, ᑎᑎᒐᓂᐊᔭᑦ ᐊᑭᑐᔪᐊᓗᕿᓚᐅᔪᒪ.
ᓂᐅᕕᐸᓚᐅᑐᒍ ᓂᐅᕕᐅᑎᑲᓯᑕ ᑕᑯᓂᒐᐅᓂᕋᑕᑎᓂ -- ᑲᓗᓇᑦ
ᓂᑭᒐᓂ ᑎᒥ, ᐸᓚᐅᒐᒥ, ᑕᑎᐅᒥ, ᐳᔪᓴᐅᑎᒥ ᐳᓂᒥᓗ.

ᐊᐅᓚᐸᓚᐅᑐᒍ ᐊᑕᐅᓯᐊᓯᑕ ᐊᐅᔭᑯᑦ ᑕᑯᔭᑐᓯᑕ ᓇᓯᑯᐱᒥ.
ᑕᓇ ᐅᒥᐊᔪᐊᒃ ᓂᐅᕕᐊᓴᓕᒪᓂᒃ ᑎᑭᐅᐳᕿᓚᐅᔪᒪᑦ ᐊᕋᒍᒪᑦ
ᓇᒪᑐᓴᓂ ᓂᐅᕕᕕᒧ. ᑯᕕᐊᓯᐸᓚᐅᑐᒍ ᑕᑯᒋᐊᓴ ᓇᓯᑯᐱᒥ.
ᐊᑕᐅᓯᒥ ᐊᕋᒍᒥ ᓇᓯᑯᐱ ᐅᔭᕋᑯᓚᐅᓯᒪᒪ ᑲᐃᒐᓯᓯᓂ ᑭᒐᓄ
ᑕᐃᒪ ᓯᕋᓚᐅᓯᒪᒪ. ᐊᒥᓯ ᐃᓄᐃ ᐱᑕᓚᐅᓯᒪᔪ ᑭᓯᑐᐃᓇᓂ
ᓯᕋᓂᑯᕕᓂᓂᒃ ᐃᑲᑎᓂᑯᕕᓂᓂ. ᐊᐅᓚᐳᔪᒐ ᐃᒃᓂᒐ ᑭᐅᒐᒃ,
ᓯᐳᔪᑕᑎᓗᒍ ᑭᐱᓂᓗ. ᑕᑯᓂᒐᒥ ᐃᓄᑲᑎᒋ ᑭᓯᑐᐃᓇᑕᑎᓗᒋ
ᑕᐃᒪ ᐃᓯᒪᓯᔪᕕᓂ ᐱᒋᐊᑲᒥᒐᒥᑕᐅᒃ.

ᑕᐃᓯᒪᓂᐅᑎᓗᒍ ᐊᒥᓯᐊᓗᐃ ᐃᓄᐃᑦ ᑭᑐᒐᑎᓗ ᐊᐅᔭᑲᓕᒪ
ᑭᒐᓂᐸᓚᐅᑐᑦ ᐊᒪᓗ ᑕᐃᒪ ᓯᓚᒐ ᑭᐅᓇᓯᒋᓂᒐᓂ, ᓄᑕᒥᒃ
ᑐᐱᕕᓴᓯᐅᐸᓚᐅᑐᑦ ᓄᓇᒥ. ᑯᕕᐊᓯᐸᓚᐅᑐᒍ ᑲᑎᒪᓕᕋᐃᒐᑕ.

got cold, they would look for new camps inland. We used
to be happy to be together. There would be dances at
the Bay residence and at the warehouse. I only danced
when I moved into the settlement after my husband died,
but there were many people in Cape Dorset then who
were good dancers. I don't remember the drum dances;
I only remember the accordion dance. They danced
Eskimo dances that went on for a long time – there were
no drunks in the dances then!

This was the old Eskimo way of life; you couldn't give up
because it was the only way. Today I like living in a house
that is always warm but, sometimes, I want to move and
go to the camps where I have been. The old life was a
hard life but it was good. It was happy.

My husband died at Natsilik. That year I hadn't wanted to
go to Natsilik and neither had Namoonie. But Ashoona
begged us to go and so we did. The week my husband
became sick we heard that his brother had died in Cape

ᑕᓂᕐᐸᓕᑕᐅᐱᓕᑕ ᓂᐅᐱᑎᑯ ᐊᖅ ᓗᓯᓂ ᐊᓪᖦ ᑭᕐᑐᐃᓇᑯᐱᒥᕐ
ᑕᓂᕐᐸᕐᑎ. ᑕᓂᕐᕐᒪᕐᒪᒐ ᑭᕐᐊᓯ ᓂᕐᒪᓚᕐᒡᒪ ᐊᖅ ᓗᖅᑐᑦᖦ
ᐅᐊᒐ ᑐᑐᓯᓇᑯᒐᓗᒐ, ᐃᓯ ᐊᒡᒐᕐᓯ ᐊᓯᓂ ᑭᓚᓂ ᑕᓂᕐᕐᑎᖦᐸ
ᓚᐅᑐᑦᖦ. ᐊᐅᓯᐱᐸᔭᕐᑐᓚ ᐊᓇᐅᓚᒐ ᑕᓂᕐᑐᓂ ᒍᒥᑐᑦᖦ;
ᐊᐅᓯᐱᔭᓚ ᑭᕐᐊᓯ ᑕᕐᔭᐊᒐ ᑕᓂᕐᑐᓂ. ᑕᓂᕐᐸᓯᐅᑐ ᐊᓇᐊ
ᑕᓂᕐᕐᕐᒥᓂ ᐊᒡᓯ ᐅᑲᕐᒍᒪᓂ –– ᐊᒥᐊᓕᒍᕐᒪᑭᖦᖕᐊᒍᒍ
ᒍᒥᑐᑦᖦ ᑕᐅᕐᒪᓯᖦ!

ᑕᓇ ᐊᓯᐊ ᐅᐸᕐᐊᑉ ᐊᐅᕐᐱᑎᕐᐊᐅᑐᒐᒪ ᕐᐱᑎᓇᐱᕐᑐ ᑕᐅᒐᓇ
ᑭᕐᐊᓇᐅᐸᐊᑕᐅᐱᓕᑦᖦ. ᓚᓇᓯ ᐊᐅᐸᖦᐅᒐᓚ ᐊᖅ ᓗᒥᒥᐊᒡᒡ ᑕᐊᓕᓪᑦᖦ
ᐅᒐᐊᑐᐊᓄᐅᒐᓚ ᐊᓯ, ᐊᓯᓇᒍ ᓂᒍᓚᐊᑐᒐ ᑐᐱᒪᕐᐊᑐᓗᓚ
ᓇᐊᓯᕐᐊᑯᐅᑐᓂᓇ. ᐊᓂᕐᑐᑦᖦ ᐊᑭᐅᐸᓯᐊᐅᑐᒐ ᐊᓯ ᐊᐅᐸᓯᐊᐅᑐᒐ.
ᑯᐊᕐᐊᖦᐸᕐᐊᐅᐱᒡᒡ.

ᐅᐊᒐ ᐊᓯᒥᕐ ᑐᑭᐅᐸᔭᒪᒪ. ᑕᓇ ᑐᑕᐅᒐ ᐊᑕᒍᑎᓚᒍᒐᓯ ᐊᓂᕐᒐ
ᒍᒍᓚᑕᐅᐱᒪᒐᓚ ᐊᖦᒐ ᑕᓇ ᐊᓚᓇᐊ ᑕᐅᓕᒍᓚᑕᐅᐱᒥᕐᓚᕐ.
ᐊᓯ ᐊᖦ ᑕᐱᓯᕐ ᑕᐅᓚᑲᑕᐅᐱᒪᒪᐅᑎᑦᖦ, ᑕᐅᓚᑕᐅᐱᒪᔭᕐᒍᑦᖦ.
ᑕᑯᐊᕐᕐᐊᓇ ᐅᐊᒐ ᑭᓇᓚᐊᕐᑕᐅᐱᑕᓇ ᐱᓇᕐᐊᑐᒥᕐ ᑐᕐᓚᐅᐱᒪᓚ

Packing a sleigh (detail).
Coloured pencil and felt pen,
ca. 1967

ᑲᑐᓈᖦ ᐅᕐᓴᑐᐅᕝ (ᐃᒪᐃᓕᒪᒐᒪ)
ᓴᖦᓱᓇ ᐊᓴᐳᓇ ᐊᒪᓗ ᐃᒪᓯᔾ
ᑎᑐᒪ, I967 ᐅᓇᔾ

Dorset, but we didn't tell Ashoona because we were afraid it would make him even sadder. He died of a very bad sickness. Many people died at that time in the camps and in Cape Dorset. There was no doctor then and nobody knew what the sickness was.

For a long time after Ashoona died we were very sad. Sometimes I thought I would lose my mind. Whenever a dog team came to the camp, Ottochie would go and look for his father. He thought he would find him.

In the spring after Ashoona died, we came out of Natsilik on a dog team. We came here to Cape Dorset just for a little while. But my relatives were no longer here. My eldest brother had died on the water; he was on a kayak and didn't return. My other brothers, with my mother who lived for a long time, had gone to Resolute Bay – some of them died around there just last year, I hear. Now I am the only one left and I often think that I will not live much longer, now that my relatives are all dead.

ᐊᒍᕝ ᓄᑲᒪ ᐅᑐᒥᐊᒪ ᑭᓗᓂ.ᐃᒍ ᐅᑲᐅᑎᓴᐅᕐᓕᒥᕐᐳᕝ
ᐊᖦᓴᓄᖦ ᑯᐱᐊᕐᕐᓴᐅᒥᐅ ᐃᓇᓂ ᐊᒍᑎᕐᔾ. ᐅᑐᓴᐅᕐᓕᔾᖦ ᐊᖦ
ᕐᐊᓄᖦ ᑲᓄᓕᕐᓇ. ᐊᕐᕐᓴ ᐃᓇᐃ ᐅᑐᓴᐅᕐᓕᕋ ᑲᐅᕐᓕᓄ
ᓄᐊᓄᓇ ᐊᓗ ᑭᓄ. ᓄᑲᖦᓇᓇᒍ ᐊᒪᓗ ᑲᐅᕝᓕᖦᖦᓇᓇᒍ
ᑲᓄᐊᔾᓇᒪᓕᖦ ᑲᓇᓗᖦ.

ᐊᒍᓇᐊᔾ ᐊᖦᕐᐊᖦ ᐅᑐᒪᓇᒍ ᑯᐱᐊᕐᕐᑐᕝᓇᐅᕐᓕᖦᒪᓕ.
ᐃᓇᓂ ᐃᕝᒪᐅᕐᖦᒍᕝᓇᐅᕐᓗᒪ. ᓇᕝᑐᖦᑲᒪᐅᒪᓗ ᑭᒍᕐᓇ ᓄᐊᓇᓇ
ᐅᖦᐅᕝ. ᓄᖦᕐᕝᓇᑐᓄᒪ ᑭᓇᕝᓴᐅᕐᐅᕝ ᐊᓄᕐᓇᖦ. ᐊᓇᕐᓇᐊ
ᐅᓇᕐᓇ ᐊᓄᕐᓇᖦ.

ᐊᖦᕐᐊ ᐅᑐᒪᓇᒍ ᐅᐃᖦᕝᖦ ᐊᐅᓄᑲᐅᕐᓕᐊᔾ ᓇᕐᓇᕐᒪᕐᓴ
ᑭᒍᕝᖦ. ᑭᑎᖦ ᑲᒪᐅᒪᑲᐃᓇᓇᐅᕐᓕᐊᔾ ᑭᓄ. ᐃᓂ ᐃᓇᑲ
ᑲᒪᓄᖦᔾᓇᐃᓇᐅᕐᓕᐊᔾ. ᐊᓇᒪ ᐊᓕᐊᕐᕝᕐ ᐅᑐᓴᐅᕐᓕᐊᔾ ᐃᒪᓇ;
ᑲᖦᐅᑐᓇ ᐅᑎᖦᓴᐅᕐᓕᕐᑐᖦ. ᐊᕐᕐᓄ ᐊᓇᖦ, ᐊᓇᓇᓗ
ᐃᓄᕐᓕᖦᐊᖦ ᐊᒍᓇᖦᓗ, ᑲᑐᕐᐊᓇᔾᕝᓕᐊᔾ ᖦᓴᐅᔾ ᐃᓇᕐᖦ
ᐅᑯᕝᓕᓇᐅ ᑲᐃᑲᓄ ᐊᖦᓇᐅᐃᓇᖦ, ᐅᖦᓇᐅᕐᓕ. ᓗᓇᓂ ᐊᕐᐊ
ᑯᐅᓇᐅᒪ ᐃᕝᒪᑲᐅᐅᒪ ᐃᓄᓇᑲᒪᕝᕐᐊᕝᓄᖦ, ᓗᓇ ᐃᓇᑲ
ᐃᓄᓇᖦᖦ ᐅᑐᒪᓇᒪᑲ.

After Ashoona died we were very poor and sometimes we would be out of oil for the kudlik. Things were given to us by other people; we used to get oil from Oshaweetok. We lived in camps near Cape Dorset and my eldest son, Namoonie, did the hunting and sometimes Kaka helped. But for a long time, we were very poor and often we were hungry. We were poor until Sowmik and the government houses came.

Before Jim Houston came to Cape Dorset we had the people at the Bay who were here for the furs, and we were grateful to have them and very pleased to be able to get tea, sugar and flour. But I think Sowmik was the first man to help the Eskimos. Ever since he came, the Eskimo people have been able to find work. Here in Cape Dorset they call him 'The Man'.

When Sowmik came to Cape Dorset we had moved into the settlement and were living here in a snowhouse. This is how we first met him. A boat was coming in from Lake

ᐊᒃᓯᓇᒃ ᑐᑯᒐᓚᑎᑐᒍ ᐊᒃᓯᐊᑐᒃ ᓯᑯᓚᐅᑐᒍᑦ ᐃᓚᓂᑐ ᐅᒃᓯᐃᒍᐸᑐᑕ ᑯᓚᒧ ᐅᒃᓯᓴᒥ. ᐊᐃᑐᑕᐅᕙᑐᑕ ᐃᓄᑲᑎᑎᓄ; ᐅᒃᓯᑕᐸᓚᐅᑐᒍ ᐅᓯᐃᑐᒥ. ᐃᒃᑐᑲᒋᑐᒥᑐᑕ ᑭᒐᐃ ᓴᓂᐊᓂ, ᐊᒪᑐ ᐊᒐᔭᓯᐸ ᐃᒃᓂᒐ ᓇᒧᓇᐃ ᐊᒍᓇᓯᐸᑐᓂ ᑲᑲᐃ ᐃᓚᓂ ᐃᑲᔭᐸᑐᓂ. ᐃᓚ ᐅᕙᓯᐊᕈᓂᐊᑐᒃ, ᓯᑯᒪᑎᐊᑐᓚᐅᑐᒍᑦ ᑭᓯᐊᓂ ᓴᐅᒥ ᑲᕙᒪᑯᑐ ᐃᒃᑐᒋ ᑎᑭᒪᑕ ᓯᑯᒍᓇᐃᓚᐅᑐᒍᑦ.

ᓴᐅᒥᒃ ᑎᑭᓚᐅᑎᓇᒍ ᑭᒐᓄᑦ ᓂᐅᕕᑎᑲᓚᐅᑐᒍᑦ ᑕᒪᓂᓚᐅᑐᓂ ᑭᓯᓄᑦ ᑎᑎᒐᓂᐊᔪᓄᑐ ᐊᒪᑐ ᑯᔪᒋᔪᐸᑐᒋᓚᐅᑕᕗ ᑕᒪᓂᒪᑕ ᓇᑯᑎᔪᐸᑐᒋᓚᐅᑕᕗ ᑎᑕᒍᓇᓚᐅᕋᑕ, ᓯᑲᒥ ᐸᓚᐅᒐᒥᑐ. ᐃᓚ ᓴᐅᒥ ᓯᕗᓕᐸᐅᓚᐅᓯᒪᑯᑐ ᐃᒃᔭᑎᐊᒐᓯᓂ ᐃᓄᓂ. ᑕᐃᒪᒐᓂ ᓴᐅᒥᒃ ᑎᑭᓚᐅᓯᒪᒪᑦ, ᐃᓄᐃᑦ ᐱᔪᓴᑕᒍᓇᓯᓯᒪᓕᑐ. ᒪᓇ ᑭᒐᒥᐅᓄᑦ ᐃᓄᓄᑦ ᐊᒍᑎᐅᓂᕋᑕᐅᔭᒃ.

ᑕᐃᓯᒪᓂ ᓴᐅᒥ ᑭᒐᓄᑎᑐᒍ ᓄᓚᐅᓯᒪᔭᒍ ᐃᒃᑐᑲᑐᒧᑦ ᐊᒪᑐ ᐃᒃᑐᕕᒐᒥᐅᒍᓚᐅᓯᒪᔭᒍ. ᑕᐃᒪᓇᑕᒐ ᑲᑎᒋᐊᒐᓚᓚᐅᓯᒪᔭᒍᒃ ᓴᐅᒥᑐ. ᑕᐃᓯᒪᓂ ᐅᒥᐊ ᑎᑭᓚᐅᓯᒪᔭ ᑭᒥᕈᒥ ᐱᓯᓂ ᑕᐃᒪ ᓂᐅᕕᐅᓚᐅᓯᒪᔭᒍ ᐃᒪᐅᑉ ᓴᓂᐊᓄ ᑕᑯᓂᐊᓯᑕ ᑭᓇᑯᒪᒐᑕ.

Bringing a gift.
Felt pen, ca. 1967

ᐊᐃᑐᑎᕐᒃ ᓇᓴᕐᔅᒃ
ᐃᒻᓕᒍ ᐊᓴᐳᑎᒍ ᑎᑐᒡ,
I967 ᐅᑎᔾ

Harbour and we went over near the Bay to see who was
on it. That was the first time I saw Sowmik. We didn't
know he was coming in and we had never heard of him
before but, immediately, he began to ask for carvings and
sewing. After this visit he came often to Cape Dorset, and
then he built his house and the government office.

At first, after Sowmik came, I did lots of sewing. I made
parkas and duffel socks with designs. Lots of women
began to work – any kind of women so long as they could
sew. I used to embroider animals and all kinds of living
things. But it was always $12 for a parka – even though
it was hard to do.

Two winters – two years – after Jim came to live in Cape
Dorset, he began to ask for drawings. Many people had
been doing the drawings before I started. It was only just
before Jim went away that I heard people were drawing to
make money. I heard that Kiakshuk was drawing, and
he was my very close relative – my mother's sister's son.

ᑕᐃᕐᒪᓂ ᑕᑯᕆᐊᓕᑦᑦᐅᕐᒪᕇᕐᓕ ᓴᐅᒻᒥ. ᑲᐅᕐᒪᐅᕐᒪᕇᑎᑦᒪ
ᑲᐃᓂᐊᒻᒪᒪ ᑐᓴᕐᐅᕐᒪᓕᒥ ᐃᒄ, ᐊᐱᑎᓴᐅᑎ ᐊᐃᓴᕐᕇᓕᕐᒃ
ᓇᒪᒍᐊᓕᓂ ᒥᕐᐅᕐᓕᕐᒍᓂ. ᓂᐅᕇᕐᒪᓕᓕᒻ ᑎᕐᒍᓇᕐᒪᕇᕐ
ᑭᓯᒻᑦ ᐊᓕᓵ ᑕᐃᒪ ᐊᕐᑐᐃᑐᐃᕐᒪᕇᕐ ᐊᕐᓱᕐᓂ ᐊᓕᓴ
ᑲᐸᓕᒃᑦ ᑎᑎᒐᐃᓂᕐᑦ.

ᕇᐳᑦᐹᕐ, ᓴᐅᕇ ᑎᑭᕐᑐᑎᒍ, ᐊᒪᕐᐸᓴᕐᒃ ᒥᕐᑎᐅᕐᒪᕇᕐ
ᒪ. ᐊᑎᕇᐅᕐᒪᒪ ᐊᓕᓴ ᐊᑎᕆᓴᓂ ᐊᓴᕆᐅᕐᒪᒪ ᑕᒃᓴᐃᑎᓴ
ᕆᑦ. ᐊᓕᓴ ᐊᒃᐃᐊᑦ ᐊᒥᕇᑦ ᒥᒃᕐᒃᑕᕐᒪᓂᕐ -- ᑭᓴᔾᐃ
ᓇᔾᑦ ᒥᒃᕇᑎᓇᑐᐊᓴᕇ. ᒥᒃᕇᑎᕐᒃ ᑕᒃᓴᐅᑎᕐᓴᐅᐅᑎᒪ
ᑲᓴᐅᑐᑐᐊᓴᓂᕐᒃ ᐅᓕᕐᔾᐊᓴᕐᒃ. ᑕᐊᓕᓕᑎᒪᕐᒃ ᐊᑎᕇᕐ ᒥᕐᓴᓂᕐ
$I2-ᑕᓴᓂ ᐊᐸᒃᐸᓴᐅᑐᕐᑦ -- ᐱᓴᑎᐊᑐᓕᓴᑐᐊᓴᕆ.

ᐅᑭᐅᓂ ᒪᕐᕃᒃ ᓴᐅᕇ ᑭᓂᓴᓕᕐᓂ ᐊᐊᑎᕇᐅᕐᒪᕇᕐ ᐱᕐᓕᕐᓂ
ᑎᑐᕐᕇᕐᒪᕐᒪᒃ. ᐊᕐᒥᔾᐊᓴᐃᑦ ᐃᓴᐃ ᑎᑎᔾᕐᑕᑕᓴᐅᕐᒪᕇᑦ
ᐱᕆᐊᓕᐅᓇᒪ. ᓴᐅᕇ ᐊᐅᑕᕇᓴᐊᕐᐱᑎᓴᒍ ᑐᓴᕐᐅᕐᒪᕇᒪ
ᐃᓴᐃᑦ ᑎᑎᒐᕐᓴᕇᐊᓴᕇ ᑭᓇᐅᕐᓴᑕᐅᑐᕐᑎᕇᕇ. ᑐᓴᕐᐅᕐᒪᕇᒪ
ᑭᐊᒃᒥ ᑎᑎᒐᕐᓴᑐᕇ ᐊᓕᓴ ᑭᐊᕐ ᐃᓴᓴᑐᕇᓴᕐᒪᕐᓴᒪ ᐊᓴᒪᓕ
ᓴᑲᓕᑦ ᐃᒃᓱᕆᓕᐅᕐᒃ.

Night demons of sky and earth.
Stone cut, 1961

ᐅᓄᐊᓄᒃ ᕿᒡᒪ ᓄ
ᐅᖜᒋ ᓐᠨᠴᒪ, 1961

Perils of the sea traveller.
Stone cut, 1960

ᐃᒪᑯᖦ ᐊᐅᖤ ᓄ ᓂᖦᐊᓄᒪ
ᐅᖜᒋ ᓐᠨᠴᒪ, 1960

Kiakshuk was drawing a lot and I wanted to do drawings, too, to make some money. I bought some paper myself and I think I made four small drawings. I think I drew little monsters. I meant the drawings to be animals but they turned out to be funny-looking because I had never done drawings before. I took these drawings to Jim's office. I was scared to go there at first but he gave me money – I think it was $20.

I began to think, maybe someday I can be like Kiakshuk. Maybe I will. Kiakshuk was working really hard on the prints when he died. He worked right up to the time he died. I am still doing the drawings and perhaps I will die like Kiakshuk, doing the drawings right up to the end.

Because Kiakshuk was a very old man, he did real real Eskimo drawings. He did it because he grew up that way, and I really liked the way he put the old Eskimo life on paper. I used to see Kiakshuk putting the shamans and spirits into his work on paper. Were the shamans useful in

ᕿᐊᠲ ᓐᠨᠴᕈ᠍ᐳᐸᐸᐲᐅᖤᒪᐦ ᑕᒪ ᓐᠨᠴᕈᒡᒪᐸᐳᐳᒪᐸᐳᐦ
ᖃᓄᐅᖤᐅᖤᒪ. ᓂᐅᐱᓯᐅᖤᒪᐦ ᐸᐃᐸᒥ ᑕᒪ ᒡᐸᑕᐅᖦᓂ
ᒥᐸᐳᓂ ᓐᠨᠴᖤᠯᐅᖤᒪᐦ. ᓐᠨᠴᖤᠯᐅᖤᒪᐦ ᑐᒡᐊᕈᓂᒪ.
ᓐᠨᠴᖦᠲ ᐅᒪᕈᐊᠯᓯᠯᔩᐊᕈᠯᠲ ᑕᒪᐊ ᐱᐅᠲᒍᐊᒍᕈᐅᖤ
ᒥᠯᐸᐧ ᓐᠨᠴᖤᠯᐅᖦᒪᐃᒪᠯ. ᑕᑯᐊ ᓐᠨᠴᖤᐊᐧ ᖤᐸᠯᐲᐧ
ᓐᠨᠴᖤᐊᠯᐅᑎᖜᖤᒪᐳᖤ ᖤᐱᐊᖤᑕᐅᖤᒪᐦ ᐅᑐᐊᠯᐊᐸ ᖦᐳᖤᒋ
ᑕᒪ $20-ᑕᒡᒥ ᖤᐱᐸᓐᑕᐅᖤᒪᕈᖤ.

ᐱᐸᐦᖤᑕᐅᖤᒪᐦ, ᐃᒪᖤ ᖤᒪᑐᐊᓄ ᕿᖤᖦ ᓯᓐᠴᒍᓄᖤᐳᖤᒋ.
ᐃᒪᖤ ᖤᐸᑐᒪ. ᕿᐊᖤᖤ ᐊᖤᕈᐊᓄ ᐱᐦᖤᐊᐳᓐᕈᒐᠯ ᓐᠨᠴᖤᓄ
ᑐᐳᖤᑕᐅᖤᒪᐧ. ᐱᐊᕈᖤᑕᐅᖤᒪᐧ ᖏᐳᖤᑕᐅᖤᕈᒪᠯᓄ ᑐᐳᖦᑕᐅᖤᐧ.
ᕈᒡ ᓐᠨᠴᖤᐸᐅᖤᖤ ᐦᐊᐅᖤ ᐃᒪᖤᐅ ᑐᐳᖤᒥᕈᐊᐧ ᕿᐊᓐᠴᒪᐧ,
ᓐᠨᠴᖤᐸᐅᓄᖤᓄᐅ ᓂᖜᐊᓄ ᓐᐱᓄᓂᐧ.

ᕿᐊᖤᖤ ᐊᐳᐊᓄᑕᐅᖤᒪᒥᐧ, ᐃᐸᕈᓐᠴᒪᓂᐧᓄ ᓐᠨᠴᖤᐸᕈᑕᐅᖤᐸᐧ.
ᑕᒪᓄᐊᐊᓄᐸᑕᐅᖤᐳᖤ ᑕᒪᓄᐊ ᐃᐸᕈᓂᒪᕈᐧ, ᐊᒡᓄ ᐱᐅᐲᖦᐸᕈᓂᐧ
ᐸᑕᐅᖤᖤ ᐊᖤᐊᕐ ᐊᖤᕈᐳᖤ ᖤᖤᓂ ᐸᐸᕐᒍᖤᐸᓂᐅᐧ. ᑕᑯᐸᑕᐅᖤᒪᐧ
ᕿᐊᖤᖤ ᐃᖤᐲᓐᒍᖔ ᐊᐧᕈ ᐳᖤᖤᓂ ᐱᐸᖤᑕᒥᓄ ᐸᐃᐸᒍᖤᐧ.

Happy family.
Engraving, 1963

ᐃᓚᒋᑦ ᖁᕕᐊᓯᑦ
ᐅᑯᓯᓴᔭᒥ ᑎᑎᑐᒐ, I963

any way? I don't know much about shamans because I don't like to think about them. Did the Anglican clergymen tell people not to be shamans? I have never heard of a single minister telling an Eskimo not to be a shaman. People just didn't like to give instructions to these powerful people.

Jim Houston told me to draw the old ways, and I've been drawing the old ways and the monsters ever since. We heard that Sowmik told the people to draw anything, in any shape, and to put a head and a face on it. He told the people that this drawing was very good. Some people saw the monsters, somewhere, some place, but I have never seen the monsters I draw. But I keep on drawing these things and, sometimes, when I take Terry a monster drawing, I say, “Perhaps when I die I'll see these monsters.”

Terry Ryan came to Cape Dorset just before Jim went away. Terry, whom we call 'The Printer', came to run the

ᐊᒐᑯᐃᑦ ᐊᑐᑐᐸᓗᕙ ᑲᓄᑐᐃᓇ? ᑲᐅᔪᒪᒋᑐᒐ ᐊᒐᑯᐃᑦ ᒥᓴᓄᑦ ᐃᓯᒪᒋᒍᒪᔭᒋᓇᑭ. ᐊᔭᑭᑐᐃᔪ ᐅᑲᐅᑎᓚᐅᐸ ᐃᓄᓂᒃ ᐊᒐᑯᑯᔪᒐᓂ? ᑐᓴᓚᐅᓯᒪᒋᓯᐊᑐᒐ ᐊᔭᑭᑐᐃᔪ ᐅᑲᑎᓗᒍ ᑕᐃᒪ ᐃᓄᓂ ᐊᒐᑯᑯᔪᒐᓂ. ᐃᓄᓄ ᒪᓕᑕᐅᑯᔪᒋᑐᐃᓇᓚᐅᓯᒪᔭᒃ ᑕᑯᓂᒐ ᓯᒍᔭᓂ ᐃᓄᓂᒃ.

ᓴᐅᒥᐅᑉ ᐅᑲᐅᑎᓚᐅᓯᒪᔭᒐ ᑎᑎᑐᔭᑯᓗᓂᒐ ᐅᕙᓯᐊᕈᓂᑕᓂᒃ, ᑕᐃᒪ ᑎᑎᑐᔭᓯᒪᔭᒐ ᐅᕙᓯᐊᕈᓂᑕᓂ ᐊᒪᓗ ᑐᒐᓂ ᑕᐃᒪᒐᓂ. ᑐᓴᓚᐅᑐᒐ ᓴᐅᒥ ᐅᑲᐅᑎᔭᕕᓂᒃ ᐃᓄᓂᒃ ᑎᑎᑐᔭᑯᔪᓯᓂ ᑲᓄᐃᑐᑐᐃᓇᓂᒃ, ᑲᓄᑐᐃᓇ ᐊᑭᓯᒪᔭᓂ, ᐊᒪᓗ ᓂᐊᑯᒐ ᐃᓕᓗᒍ ᑭᓇᑲᑎᓗᒍᓗ. ᐅᑲᐅᑎᓚᐅᑐ ᐃᓄᓂᒃ ᑕᓇ ᓂᐊᑯᑲᑐᒃ ᑭᓇᑲᓯᓂᓗ ᑎᑎᑐᔭ ᐊᒃᓯᐊᓗ ᐱᐅᔭᐸᓗᓚᐅᑐ. ᐃᓄᐃᑦ ᐃᓚᒋ ᑕᑯᓚᐅᑐ ᑐᒐᓂ, ᓇᒥᑐᐃᓇ, ᓄᓇᒥ ᐃᓚ ᑕᑯᓚᐅᓯᒪᔭᒋᑕᓂᒃ ᑐᒐᓂ ᑎᑎᑐᔭᐸᑐᒐ. ᐃᓚ ᑎᑎᑐᔭᒋᓇᑲᑕᑐᒐ ᑕᑯᓂᒐ ᐊᒪᓗ ᐃᓚᓂᑯ ᑎᐅᑎᒧᓯᓕᒐᒪ ᑐᒐᓂ ᑎᑎᑐᔭᓯᒪᔭᓂ ᐅᑲᓗᒐ "ᐃᒪᑲ ᑐᑯᒍᒪ ᑕᑯᓚᑕᑲ ᑕᑯᐊ ᑐᒐᐃᑦ". ᑎᐅᑎ ᕿᐃᔭᓐ ᑭᒐᓄᓚᐅ

Some people saw the monsters,
somewhere, some place.
Felt pen, 1970

ᐃᓄᐃᑦ ᐃᓕᒥᑦ ᑕᑯᕐᒪᔮᑦ ᑐᓗᓂᒃ
ᓇᓂᑐᐃᓇ ᐊᑕᐅᑎᒍᑦ ᐊᓚᒥᒍᑦ ᑎᑎᒐ
I 970

Bird spirit and fish.
Stone cut, 1968

ᑯᐸᓄᐊᖅ ᐊᒻᓗ ᐃᖃᓗᖅ
ᐅᖅᓯᒥ ᑎᑎᒐ, I 968

Co-op. The Co-op sends the carvings and prints to the
south, and it is owned by Eskimos. I don't know exactly
how it works but there is a board of directors who are
Eskimo. Terry gives out the pens and the papers for
drawing, and later when we bring him our work, he pays
for the drawings and carvings. I don't do drawings when
Terry has gone somewhere; when Terry's away I get
tired of waiting for him. A lot of people miss him when
he's away.

Since the Co-op began I have earned a lot of money with
my drawing. I get clothes from the drawings, and I earn
a living from paper. Because Ashoona, my husband
is dead I have to look after myself, and I am very grateful
for these papers – papers we tear so easily. Whenever
I am out of everything, I do some drawings and I take them
to Terry at the Co-op and he gives me money with which
I can buy clothes and tea and food for the family. He is
paying well. I am happy to have the money and I am glad
we have a Co-op.

ᓯᒪᐊ ᓴᐅᒥ ᐊᐅᓚᕐᒐ-ᐊᖕᓯᐱᑎᓂᒍᒍ. ᑎᑎᐱ ᑕᓇ ᐊᖅᕐᖃᑕᐅ
ᑎᑎᒐᑕ ᑎᖃᐱᐅᕐᒪᐊᖅ ᒍᕐᐊᑕᒥ ᖃᒪᕐᐊᑐᕐᓂᓐ. ᑕᓇ ᒍᕐᐊᖅ
ᐊᐅᓚᑎᕐᖃᑕᑐ ᓴᐅᐱᓐᓂᒐ ᑎᑎᒐᓕᒍᒐ ᖃᒐᓇᑦ ᖃᐊᓚᒐ, ᐊᒻᓗ
ᖃᒥᓂᖅᐅᐅᓂᒐ ᐃᓄᐃᑦ. ᖃᐅᐱᒪᕐᒐᒍ ᖃᓇᕐᐊ ᐱᓯᒍᓐᒐ ᐃᓕ
ᐊᓚᑐᖃᒐ ᐃᓄᓂᐅ. ᑎᑎᐱ ᑐᓂᖅᖃᑕ ᑎᑎᖅᐊᑎᓂᑐᑦ ᐸᐊᓚᒐᐅ
ᑎᑎᒐᕐᐊᓯᓂ ᐊᒻᓗ ᐊᕐᒐᖃᖅᑕᓇ ᑎᑎᒐᕐᓂ ᖃᐊᒍᐊᓚᒍᐅ.
ᑎᑎᒐᕐᖃᑕᖅᑐᖅᑐᒐ ᑎᑎᐱ ᐊᐅᓚᕐᒐᓚᐊᒐ ᖃᓚᐅᐊᖄ; ᑎᑎᐱ
ᐊᐅᓚᕐᒐᓚᐅᒐᒐᓚᑦ ᐅᖅᒍᐊᒍᕐᒐ. ᐃᓄᐃᑦ ᐊᒥᕐᓂᖅ ᐱᐊᖃᖃᐅᐊ
ᓯᒐᖃᑐᖅ ᐊᐅᓚᕐᒐᓚᐅᒐᓚᑦ.

ᑕᐅᓚᒐᓂ ᒍᕐᐊᖅᐊᔮᖅ ᐱᓯᒐᐱᖃᐅᐱᒐᓚᑦ ᖃᐱᐅᖅᐊᑐᒐᖃᐅᓚᑦ
ᑎᑎᒐᐱᖃᐅᓂᑐᑦ. ᐊᐅᖃᖅᖃᖅᐱᓚ ᑎᑎᒐᐱᖃᐅᓂᑐᑦ, ᐊᒻᓗ ᖃᐅᐱᖅᖃᐊᐅ
ᐃᓄᒐᓚ ᐸᐊᐱᒐ. ᐅᐊᓚ ᑐᒍᓚᖃᓚ ᐊᒥᓂ ᖃᒪᕐᐊᐱᓚᓚ ᐊᒻᓗ
ᖃᒍᖅᑐᓚ ᑕᒍᒍᓚ ᐸᐊᐱᒐ ᐊᕐᐱᐊᑕᐱᐊᖅᐱᐊᕐᐊᖃᐊ. ᐱᓚᐅ ᐃᒐᕐᒐᓚ
ᖃᒍᕐᒐᓚᓚ ᐱᕐᐱᓚᐃᒐᐊᖃᐊᖅ, ᑎᑎᒐᐱᒍᖅᐱᐱᓚ ᑕᐊᓚ ᑎᑎᐱᑐᒐᓚᕐᒐᖅᑦᑎᑕ
ᒍᕐᐊᖅᐱᐱᑐ ᐸᐊᐱᕐᓂ ᖃᐅᕐᖃᖅᐱᐱ ᐊᖃᒐᖃᓇ ᓂᐅᐊᐅᑎᖄᖃᐱᓇ ᑎᒐᐱ
ᐃᐊᓚᖃᐅ ᓇᑎᕐᖃᒪᕐ. ᑎᑎᐱ ᐊᐱᐊᓚᐊᐊᕐᖃᐅᓚᐅᖃᕐᖃ. ᒍᑯᐊᖅᑐᓚ
ᐱᖃᐅᕐᖃᐱᐊᒍᐱ ᐊᒻᓗ ᖃᒍᕐᒐᓚ ᒍᕐᐊᖅᐊᕐᐱᓚᑕ.

The woman with the blue fish spear.
Felt pen, 1970

ᐊᑳᓄᖕ ᑐᒍᐊᑎᒻᖕ ᖃᑉᕿᓇᖕ
ᐃᓚᒍ ᐊᓚᐅᓄᒍ ᓐᓇᑐᒪ, I 970

Pitseolaks.
Felt pen, 1970

ᐱᕈᐅᓚᕝ
ᐃᓚᒍ ᐊᓚᐅᓄᒍ ᓐᓇᑐᒪ, I 970

Does it take much planning to draw? Ahalona! It takes much thinking, and I think it is hard to think. It is hard like housework.

The other day I drew an Eskimo woman with a blue fish spear. I did not want to leave the fish spear alone; that is why I put the bird on her head. There's a baby hidden inside the parka, too – you can tell by the shape of the parka!

When I first started doing the drawings I did all the work in black and brown, and I still like these two colours, although now we are using many coloured pens. Jim said to draw the old ways in bright colours.

After Terry gets the drawings, some are put on the stone and made into prints. The drawings are carved into stone by Nawpachee's husband, Eegyvudluk, and by Iyola, Lukta and Ottochie. After they are put on the stone, they are always better. Sometimes we make prints, too, with

ᓐᓇᑐᖕᓚᒪᒥᐊᒥ ᐱᖕᓇᐊᑐᖕᑊ! ᐊᖃᓗᓇ! ᒪᓐᐊᒍᖕ ᐊᖕᒡᐊᒍ.
ᐊᒡᒪᒥᐊᑲᖕᓗ ᐅᖃᒪ ᐊᒡᒪᒥᐊᑲᖕᓗᒍᖕᖕᒪ. ᐱᖕᓇᐊᑐᖕᐊᖃᓗ
ᐊᖕ ᓗᓂᖕᓐᐊᖃᓄᑐᖕᑊ.

ᐅᓗᐊ ᐊᓚᓗᓇ ᓐᓇᑐᖕᓚᖃᐅᒥᖕᒍ ᐊᓄᒥ ᐊᖃᓇᒥ ᑐᒍᐊᖃᓄᒍ
ᐊᖃᓗᒥ ᖃᖕᖃᐊᖕᑐᒥ. ᐊᖃᐅᑐᐊᑐᖃᐅᒥᐊᑯ ᐊᖃᓗᒥ ᖃᖕᖃᐊᓄ,
ᑕᐊᒪᐊᒪᖕᑊ ᓂᐊᖃᓗᓇᑐᖃᐅᒍ ᒍᖃᓂᒪᖃ. ᐱᐊᖅᑯ ᓂᒪ
ᐊᖃᓄᒪᖃᑐᑕᐅᖃ ᐊᓄᖃᐊᖃ ᐊᓄᐊᓇ, ᑕᑲᖃᐊᖃ ᐊᖃᓄᒪᓇᓄ
ᐊᓄᖃᐊᖃ !

ᓐᐊᖃᒪ, ᓐᓇᑐᖕᖃᑕᑕᐊᐊᓂᒪ ᓐᓇᖃᑐᖃᖕ ᐊᓗᓇᖕ
ᖃᓂᑕᐅᐊᐊᑐᑊ ᖃᑐᓇ ᐊᐊᓄ ᒪᓂ ᑕᑲᐊ ᒪᐅ ᒪᒍᐊᐅᓐᖕ
ᐱᐅᖃᓂᐊᖃᖕ, ᒪᓇ ᐊᒥᓇ ᐊᐅᓇᐊᖃᐅᒪ ᑕᖃᓇᓇᖕ ᓐᓇᑐᖃ
ᐅᓇᖕᖕ.

ᓐᐊᓇ ᐊᒥᖃᒪᕞᐊᒪ ᓐᓇᑐᖕᖕᒪᐊᓇ ᐊᓗ ᐅᖃᒍᐊᑐᐊᖕᓗᓇ
ᐊᒪᓗ ᓐᓇᑐᖕᖃᐊᓇᖕᐊᓗᓇ. ᑕᑲᐊ ᓐᓇᑐᖃᒪᕞᐊᖕ ᖃᓂᖃᒪᕞᐊᖕ
ᐅᖃᒍᐊᖕ ᓇᐊᐅᖃᑊ ᐅᐊᓗᓇ, ᐊᓄᐊᖕᓗᒍᒪ, ᐊᒪ ᐊᐊᐅᑎᒪᑊ,
ᓄᖕᑕ ᐅᓄᖃᒥᓗᓇ. ᑕᑲᐊ ᓐᓇᑐᖃᕞᐊᒪᖃᐅᓇᒥᒥ ᖃᖕ ᖃᓂᐅᓇᓐᓇ
ᖃᒡᓇᓗᓇ ᐅᖃᒍᐊᑐᖃᒪᑕᒥᒪ, ᑕᐊᒪᒪᒪ ᐊᐊᐅᓇᐊᖃᑐᑊ.

Girl on a windy day.
Coloured pencil and felt pen,
ca. 1967

ᓂᕕᐊᓯᐊᒃ ᐊᓄᕆᓯᐅᑦ
ᑕᒃᓴᓂᓄ ᐊᓚᐅᑎᓄ ᐊᒪᓗ ᐃᒪᓂᒧᑦ
ᑎᑎᑐᒐ, 1967 ᐅᑎᓗᒍ

stencils and with copper plates. Now some of the drawings are also arranged on material and, when it is carefully done, it looks very well.

Sometimes, when I see pictures in books of my drawings and prints, I laugh. I laugh to think they have become something. But even when they are waiting for papers from the south, Terry Ryan is giving artist's papers to me. Sometimes, when I am the only one who is given papers to draw on, I am scared that the other women will become jealous of me. Sometimes I feel sorry when other people don't have papers – papers which I can get.

But many Cape Dorset people have done well with the prints. I don't know who did the first print, but Kiakshuk, Niviaksiak, Oshaweetok and Tudlik were all drawing at the beginning. I liked the first prints – I liked them because they were truly Eskimo. Others have worked well, too. Parr was an old man when he began to draw, and he died last year, but I really loved the way he drew. Kenojuak

ᒪᓇ ᑎᑎᑐᖅᓯᒪᔪᐃ ᐃᓚᖏ ᐊᑭᑕᐅᓯᒪᒥᔪᑕᐅ ᑲᓗᓇᑕᒎ ᐊᒪᓗ ᐱᓯᐊᓯᒪᑐᐊᒐᒥ, ᐱᓯᐊᓯᒪᔪᐸᓗᑲᑕᑦ.

ᐃᓚᓂ, ᑕᑯᒐᒪ ᐊᐳᒍᐊᓂ ᐅᑲᓕᒪᒐᒥᑐᓂ ᑎᑎᑐᖅᑕᕕᓂᓂᕋ ᑎᑎᑐᖅᒎᓯᒪᔪᓂᓗ, ᐃᔪᐸᑐᒐ. ᐃᔪᐸᑐᒐ ᐃᓯᒪᓯᒐ ᑕᑯᐊ ᓯᓇᑐᐃᓇᒎᕆᐊᕆ. ᐃᓚ ᐅᑕᑭᑲᓗᐊᒪᑕ ᐸᐃᐸᓂ ᑲᓗᓇ ᓄᓇᒐᓂ ᐱᔪᓂ, ᑎᐅᕆᐅᑉ ᐊᐃᑐᐸᑕᒐ ᑎᑎᑐᖅᑎᐅᑉ ᐸᐃᐸᒐᓂ. ᐃᓚᓂ ᐅᕋᒐ ᑭᓯᐊᓂ ᐸᐃᐸᒥᒃ ᐊᐃᑐᑕᐅᖅᖁᐃᒐᒪ ᑎᑎᑐᖅᕕᓴᒥᒃ ᑲᐱᐊᓯᐸᑐᒐ ᐊᓯᒃ ᐊᒃᓇᐃ ᐱᐳᓗᓴᓴᓂᐊᒪᑕ ᐅᕋᓂ. ᐃᓚᓂ ᒪᒥᐊᐸᑐᒐ ᐊᓯᒃ ᐃᓄᐃᑦ ᐸᐃᐸᒃᒍᓇᐃᑐᐊᒪᑕ ᐸᐃᐸᒥ ᐅᕋᒐ ᐱᔭᓇᑕᒐᓂ.

ᐃᓚ ᐊᒥᓱ ᑭᒐᒥᐅ ᐃᓄᐃᑦ ᐱᓯᐊᓯᒪᔪᓂ ᑎᑎᑐᖅᓕᐅᓯᒪᔪᑦ. ᑲᐅᐳᒪᕆᑐᒐ ᑭᓇ ᓯᕗᓕᐸᐅᓯᓂ ᑎᑎᑐᖅᓯᒪᔪᓕᐅᓂᒪᒐ, ᐃᓚ ᑭᐊᓯ ᓂᕕᐊᓯᐊᒃ, ᐅᓯᐃᑐ ᑐᓕᓗ ᐃᓗᓇᑎᒃ ᑎᑎᑐᖅᓯᒪᔪᓕᒪ ᓯᕗᓕᒥ ᐱᕆᐊᒐᓯᑎ. ᐱᐅᓴᑐᒐ ᓯᕗᓕᒥ ᑎᑎᑐᖅᒎᓯᒪᑲᑐᕕᓂᓂ ᐱᐅᕆᖅᑲ ᐃᓄᓕᑎᐅᕈᓕᐅᒪᑕ. ᐊᓯᕆ ᐱᓯᐊᐸᓕᐅᒥᔪᐃᑕᐅᒃ. ᐸ ᐃᑐᐊᓗᓕᐅᑐ ᑎᑎᑐᖅᓕᓴᓯᓂ ᐊᒪᓗ ᑐᑯᓕᐅᑐ ᐊᖁᓂ, ᐃᓚ ᐱᐅᕆᖅᐸᓗᕆᓕᐅᑕᒃ ᑎᑎᑐᖁᒍᓯᕆᕈᓕᐅᑕᒐ. ᐊᒪᓗ ᑭᓄᐊᔪᐊᑉ ᐅᒃᐱᓕᐊᒐ ᑐᓴᓕᐅᑐᒐ ᐱᓇᓕᖅᐅᓯᔪᕕᓂᒥ ᑲᓗᓇ ᓄᓇᒐᓂ.

Woman hiding from spirit.
Stone cut, 1968

ᐊᑲᓂᒃ ᑐᒥᓐᐸ ᐃᐱᓯᒪᖅ
ᐅᕿᒋ ᓐᑐᒪ, 1968

made the owl which, I hear, became famous in the south. Lucy is good sometimes and I have seen something of Pudlo's which I like.

My children are working for the Co-op, too. Kaka and Kiawat are carving. Kiawat has also done prints — he once drew a muskox with big horns — but he has been carving since he was a young boy and is good at the carving. Kaka also makes good money carving. Nawpachee does sewing, drawing and carving, and Kumwartok and Ottochie and Namoonie carve sometimes. But Kaka and Kiawat are best. Once, Kiawat and Nawpachee's husband, Eegyvudluk, went to Ottawa to do some carving and meet the Queen. Jim Houston arranged it. But they didn't go to Frobisher Bay to see her there when she came this year. They had seen her already.

I know I have had an unusual life, being born in a skin tent and living to hear on the radio that two men have landed on the moon. I think the new times started for Eskimos

ᓘᐱᐅᔅ ᓐᑐᔅᒪᑎᕐ ᐱᐅᐊᕐᒥᔪ, ᑕᑯᕆᒪᕋᒪ ᐱᑲᑐᐊᒥᒃ
ᐸᕐᓗ ᓐᑐᔅᑲᓐᕿᐅᒥᒃ ᐱᐅᕐᑕᐅᔨᐅᒃ, ᐊᒧ ᐱᐅᓴᑐᒪ
ᕿᖃᓴᕕ ᓐᑐᔅᒪᔾᐊᐅ ᑲᓐᕆᐅᔅ ᓐᑐᔅᑲᓐᕿᐅᒥᒃ.

ᕿᑐᒃᑲ ᐃᖃᓂᐅᔅᕆᔾ ᔪᐅᐊᑯᕆ. ᑲᑲ, ᕿᐅᓚᑐ ᓇᐅᐱᑐ.
ᕿᐅᓘᒃ ᓐᑐᔅᕆᓚᔾᔪᑕᐅᒃ ᐊᐸᕆᓚᕐᒃ ᐊᑕᐅᕐᐊᓯᐅ ᓐᑐ
ᔅᕆᓚᕐᒃ ᐅᒥᓗᖃᒃ ᐊᕐᕐᐊᒍᕆ ᖃᔪᓐᐊᔪ -- ᐃᐃ
ᓇᔪᐊᕐᓚᖃᑐ ᑕᐊᓪᓗᓴ ᕐᔅᐳᑲᐅᕐᓗᒥᕐ ᐊᒧ ᐱᕐᐊᖅᑐᒃ
ᓇᔪᐊᑕᕐᓴ. ᑲᑲᔅᑕᐅ ᕿᓇᐅᖅᑕᐅᕐᐊᖃᑕᕐᕐᔅᒃ ᓇᔪᐊᓪᓴ.
ᓇᐸᕐ ᒥᕐᐸᖅᒃ ᓐᑐᔅᕐᓴᓴ ᓇᐅᓪᕐᓴᓴ ᐊᒧ ᑯᓪᐊᔅ
ᐅᑐᕿᓴ ᐊᐅᕐᐊᐊᓴ ᓇᐅᕐᕆᕐᕐ ᐃᓴᓂᔪ. ᐃᐃ ᑲᑲ ᕿᐅᓘᒃ
ᐱᕐᐊᕐᔪᓴᐊᕐ. ᐊᑕᐅᕐᐊᐊᓐᑎ, ᕿᐅᓘᔅᓴ ᓇᐊᕐᐸᐅᓴ ᐅᐊᒪ,
ᐃᐅᕐᓴᓴ, ᐊᔪᐊᐅᐊᐃᒪᓚᕐ ᓇᔪᐊᐊᓐᐊᔪᕐᑎ ᑕᑯᕆᐊᔪᕐᕐ
ᔪᐊᐅᕐᒃ ᐊᑯᓴᐊᓴᕐ. ᐲᕆ ᕐᐲᑕᐅᔅ ᑕᐊᓪᐊᐃᓐᑕᐅᕐᓴᐅᕐᔅ.
ᐃᐃ ᐃᖃᓴᓄᑲᐅᕐᐊᔪᔅ ᑕᑯᕐᔅᐳᕐᔪ ᑕᐊᔪᒪ ᓐᑎᓐᓴᔪ ᓚ
ᐅᕿᐅᒃ ᑕᑯᕐᕐᐸᓚᓴᕐᕐᐅᒃ.

ᑲᐅᕐᓚᕐᒪ ᐊᐅᐱᒥᑐᕐ ᐃᖏᕐᑲᐃᐊᕐᒃ, ᐃᖏᓂᐊᖏᐅᕐᒪ
ᕿᕐᒥ ᔪᐊᒥ ᐊᒧ ᐃᖏᒪ ᔪᓐᑲᕐᒪ ᖃᓐᑕᐅᔪ ᒪᖅ ᐊᔪᓐ
ᓄᐊᕐᒪᔅᓐᐊᕐ ᑕᕿᒧ. ᓄᑎᕐ ᐊᕐᐊᕐᓚᕐᐊᓐᕐᔅᒪ ᐃᖃᓄ ᑲᖃᓇ

Caribou and birds.
Stone cut, 1963

The knives, the drying rack,
the things we made to use.
Felt pen, 1970

ᑐᑐᒃ ᐊᒻᒪ ᑯᕐᓗᐊᖅ
ᐅᖅᓯᒥ. ᑎᑎᕈᒪ, 1963

ᓴᕕᐊᑦ, ᐸᓂᕐᕕᐊᒃ, ᓴᕙᑦᐳ(ᔅᐸ ᐊᑐ
ᓂᐊᔪᒥ ᐊᒪᓕᒍ ᐊᑕᐅᑎᒍ ᑎᑎᕈᒪ,
1970

after the white people's war, when the white men began to
make many houses in the Arctic. Eskimos began to move
into the settlements and then the white people started
helping us to get these houses. That's why life changed.
I don't think everybody was too fond of moving from
the camps, but they still came anyway. Now they just
stay here in Cape Dorset. They are working for the white
man now.

Kaka didn't want to move away from his camp so now his
camp has a real house. He had it moved down the shore.

In some ways I like living in a warm house, but in the old
days, before all these things happened, we were always
healthy. I was never sick, not even with all the children
I had. In these late years I have been sick most of the
time and I have felt each year harder to bear. Now that we
all live in one place we get sick a lot. My worry now
is over one of my sons who was very sick in the spring. He
is down south now and I do not know how he is doing.

ᐅᓇᑦᑎᕆᓕᓴᑎᓱᒥ, ᑲᖐ ᐊᒡᒥᓂ ᐊᒃ ᓄᑰᑎ ᐊᕐᓚᑐᕐᒪᖏᑦ
ᐊᓄᐊᑦ ᓄᐊᓗᓂ. ᐊᓄᐊᑦ ᓄᕐᑲᑎ ᐊᕐᓚᑐᕐᒪᖐ ᐊᒃ ᓄᖃᒍᑎ
ᐊᒻᒪ ᑕᐅᒻ ᑲᓴᐅᑦ ᐊᒃᕙᑎ ᐊᕐᓚᑐᕐᒪᖐᑦ ᐅᕐᓯᓂ ᑕᑯᓂ
ᐊᒃ ᓄᒃᑲᑖᕐᓂᖅ. ᑕᐅᒻᐊᒻ ᐊᓄᕐ ᐊᕐᓂᖅᓯᓚᑐᖅᑦ. ᐊᓄᓂᒻᒃ
ᐊᑯᕐᓯᐊᑐᑯᕐᑎ ᓂᕐᐊᒃ ᓄᕐᒥᓂ, ᐊᑎ ᑎᕐᑯᐊᓂᑲᑐᐊᑦ.
ᒪᑎ ᑕᒻᐊᑐᐊᓂᑐ ᑭᓂᒥ. ᐊᒃᓇᐊᕐᑯᑐᑎᓂ ᑲᓴᓂᒪ.

ᑲᒃ ᓄᒍᓚᑐᕐᓂ ᓄᓂᒥ ᑕᐅᒻ ᒪᓂ ᓄᐊᒻ ᐊᓱᑐᑦᑲᑐᐊᓄᑦ.
ᑲᒃᐳᑦ ᓄᑕᐅᑉᐊᓂᑲᐳᑕᓄᒃ ᕐᓯᒍᑦ.

ᐊᓄᒻᒍᑦ ᐳᐅᓱᑐᒻ ᐅᑯᕐᕐᕐᐊᕐᒃ ᐊᒃ ᓂᒻ ᐊᑎ ᐅᕐᐸᐊᐳ
ᑕᒻᒍᐊᑖᒪ ᐊᑐᓂᑐᖐᒥ, ᑕᐅᒻᒪᓂ ᑲᓄᐊᐸᓄᕐᒍᒻᕐᐳᑎ.
ᑲᓂᒪᑦᐸᑐᐳᓂᒻ, ᑕᑐᑎᓂᑐᒻᒐᓄᓂ ᑭᑐᑲᕐᓂᒻ. ᐊᒍᒍᑦ
ᐅᑐ ᑲᓂᒪᐊᓄᑐᓂᒻ ᐊᒻᒪ ᐊᒍᒍᑕᑦ ᑲᓂᒪᓚᐳᕐᕐᓱᐸᕐᒻᒻ.
ᒪᓂ ᐊᓄᒻᑎ ᐊᑲᐳᕐᒻᕐᓂᒻᕐ ᑲᓂᒪᓱᐊᕐᓂᑐᒍ. ᐊᕐᒻᓂᕐᑉᒻ
ᒪᓂ ᐊᓂᒍᔪᕐᒻᓂᑐᒃ ᐊᒃᓂᒻ ᐊᓂᒪ ᑲᓂᕐᕐᕐᑎᐊᓱᓂᕐᒻ ᐅᐊᑎ
ᕐᒃ. ᑲᐐ ᓄᐊᓗᒍᑐ ᒪᓂ ᑲᐅᕐᓂᕐᑐᒪ ᑲᓂᐊᕐᓚᓄᑦ.

The little owl.
Stone cut, 1968

ᐅᒃᐱᐊᐱᒃ
ᐅᔭᕋᒥ ᑎᑎᑐᒐ, 1968

Fishing in front of the snow shelter.
Felt pen, ca. 1967

ᓯᑯᒥ ᐊᐅᓚᓴᑐᒃ ᐊᐳᑎᒥᒃ ᐅᑯᐊᑲᓯᓂ
ᐃᒪᓕᒧ ᐊᓚᐅᑎᒧ ᑎᑎᑐᒐ,
1967 ᐅᑎᓗᒍ

A few years ago, too, there was a great loss in our family. Nawpachee and her husband, Eegyvudluk, were at church and they left their young children at home. The house caught fire and they died.

But I think the new ways would be better than the old, except that nowadays the young people make so much trouble. A long time ago when I was bringing up my children they would do what you told them to do. If you gave them something to eat they were grateful and happy about it. Ottochie, especially, was always thankful for everything. If he asked to do something and I said yes, he'd be really pleased; if I said no, he wouldn't do it. Now, all that has changed. They don't listen at all. People get worse when they all live in one place. The young people are always in trouble; if they were out of trouble, it would be much better the new way.

I have heard there is someone – not a human being but a spirit – in the moon. When I heard that the two men had

ᐊᒪᓗᑕᐅ ᐅᑭᐅᑦ ᐊᒥᓯᒋᑐ ᐊᓂᒍᓯᒪᓕᑐ ᐃᓚᐃᑐᐸᓗᓚᐅᑐᒍᑦ
ᓇᐸᓯ ᐅᐃᒐᓗ, ᐃᐯᓗᐊᔪ ᑐᓯᐊᕕᓕᐊᓯᑎ ᐱᐊᕋᒥᓂ ᑭᒪᐃᔪᕕ
ᓂᑦ ᑲᑲᐅᓗ ᐸᓂᒐᓂ, ᑕᒪᓂᓕᐅᓯᒪᔪᒥ ᐃᓕᓴᓯᓂ ᑭᒐᓂ,
ᐊᓂᕋᓂ. ᐃᒃ ᓗ ᐃᑯᐊᓕᓂᒪ ᑕᐃᒪ ᑕᑯᐊ ᑐᑯᓕᐅᔪᔪᑦ.

ᐃᓚ ᓄᑕᑎᑐᑦ ᐱᐅᓂᓴᐅᔪᕆᓯᔪᒐ ᐅᐯᓯᐊᕈᓂᑕᒥᒥᒃ, ᑭᓯᐊᓂ
ᒪᓇᐅᓕᑐ ᐅᕕᑲᐃᑦ ᐊᒃᓯᐊᓗ ᐱᒐᓚᑲᑕᓕᑐ. ᐅᐯᓯᐊᕈᐊᓗᒃ
ᐱᐊᕋᑲ ᐱᐊᕋᐅᑎᓗᒋ ᐊᒐᓯᐊᐸᓚᐅᑐ ᐅᑲᐅᑎᒐᑭ. ᐊᐃᑐᒐᑭᑦ
ᓯᓇᑐᐃᓇᒥ ᓂᕆᒐᓴᒥ ᓇᑯᓴᐸᓚᐅᑐ ᑯᕕᐊᒋᓯᒋᓗ. ᐅᒃᑐᑭ,
ᐱᓗᐊᑎᓗᒍ. ᑕᐃᒪᒐ ᓯᕆᔪ ᓯᓇᓕᒪᓂ. ᓯᓇᑐᐃᓇᓕᕆᒍᒪᓯᓂ
ᐊᐱᕆᑐᐊᒪᑦ ᑕᐃᒪ, ᐊᒋᒐᑯ, ᐊᒃᓯᐊᓗᒃ ᑯᕕᐊᓯᐸᓚᐅᑐᒃ;
ᐊᒋᒋᑐᐊᒐᒪ, ᑲᒪᓂᐅᔭᒐᓂ. ᒪᓇᓕ ᐃᓗᓇᑎ ᑕᐃᒪᐃᒍᓇᐃᐳ.
ᓇᓚᒋᓯᐊᓕᑐ. ᐃᓄᐃ ᐱᐯᓕᐊᑐᐃᓇᑐ ᐃᓗᓇᑎ ᐊᑕᐅᓯᓴᐃᓇᒥ
ᓄᓇᑲᓕᑐᐊᒐᒥ. ᐅᕕᑲᐃ ᑕᐃᒪᒐᓕᒪ ᐱᒐᓚᐸᑐ ᐱᒐᓚᑲᑕᒋᐸᑕ
ᐱᐅᓂᓴᐸᓗᒐᔭᑐ ᓄᑕᒍᓕᑐ ᐱᐅᓯᒃ.

ᑐᓴᓯᒪᔪᒐ ᑭᓇᑐᐃᓇᑲᑐᒥ ᐃᓄᒋᑐ ᐃᓚ ᑐᒐ -- ᑕᑭᒥᑐᒃ.
ᑐᓴᕋᒪ ᐊᒍᑎᒃ ᒪᕈ ᓄᓇᑐᕕᓂᐅᒋᐊᒋ ᑕᑭᒧ. ᐃᓯᒪᔪᔪᒐ

In summer we hunted dulse
on the beach.
Felt pen, ca. 1967

ᐊᐅᔭᒥ ᑭᒍᐊᔪᐸᓪᓚᑐᒍ ᓴᔾᒥ
ᐊᒪᓪᒍ ᐊᓚᐅᑎᒍ ᑎᑎᕐᒪ,
I967 ᐅᑎᓪᒍ

Fishing through the ice.
Coloured pencil and felt pen,
ca. 1967

ᓯᓪᒥ ᐊᐅᓚᓯᑐᖅ
ᑕᖅᓯᓴᓄ ᐊᓚᐅᑎᓄ ᐊᒪᓪᒍ ᐊᒪᓪᒍᑦ
ᑎᑎᕐᒪ, I967 ᐅᑎᓪᒍ

Spirit of happy women.
Coloured pencil and felt pen,
ca. 1967

ᐊᒃᓇᐅᑉ ᑯᕕᐊᓯᓂᒐ
ᑕᒃᓴᓕᓄ ᐊᓚᐅᑎᓄ ᐊᒪᓗ ᐃᒪᓕᒧᑦ
ᑎᑎᑐᒐ, 1967 ᐅᑎᓗᒍ

landed on the moon I wondered what the spirit thought of these two men landing on his land.

ᑲᓄ ᑐᒐᒃ ᐃᓯᒪᓂᒪᒐᑦ ᑕᑯᓂᒐ ᐊᒍᑎᓂ ᒪᕈᓂ ᓄᓇᑐᓂᒃ, ᓄᓇᒐᓄᑦ.

We have an Anglican church here in Cape Dorset and every Sunday I go there. The missionaries came to the Arctic a long time ago and I was married by the Anglican clergyman, Inutaquuq. But for a long time we had no church in Cape Dorset. Then Pootagook, the father of Eegyvudluk, Nawpachee's husband, told the missionaries that they should bring a church to Cape Dorset. He said the Eskimos would give fox skins to pay for materials.

ᑐᓯᐊᕕᑲᑐᒧᑦ ᐊᔪᑭᑐᐃᕗᑯᑦ ᑐᓯᐊᕕᒐᓂ ᒪᓂ ᑭᒐᓂ ᐊᒪᓗ ᐊᓕᑎᐊᑕᒪ ᑕᐃᑯᒐᐸᑐᒐ. ᐊᔪᑭᑐᐃᕗ ᐃᓄᐃ ᓄᓇᒐᓄᓚᐅᓯᒪᔪ ᐅᕙᓯᐊᕈᐊᓗ ᐊᒪᓗ ᑲᑎᑎᑕᐅᓯᒪᔪᒐ ᐊᔪᑭᑐᐃᕗᒧ ᐃᓄᑕᒍᒧ. ᐃᓚ ᐅᕙᓯᐊᕈᓂᓂᐊᓗ ᑐᓯᐊᕕᑲᓚᐅᕆᑐᒍ ᑭᒐᓂ. ᑕᐃᒪ ᐳᑐᒍ ᐃᕙᓗᐊᔪᑉ ᐊᑕᑕᒐ, ᓇᐸᓯᐅᓗ ᐅᐃᒐ, ᐅᑲᐅᑎᓚᐅᓯᒪᔪᒃ ᐊᔪᑭᑐᐃᕗᓂᒃ ᑐᓯᐊᕕᑕᑲᐃᔪᓴᐅᕆᐊᕆᓂ ᑭᒐᓂ. ᐅᑲᓚᐅᓯᒪᔪ ᐃᓄᐃ ᑐᓂᓯᑲᑕᓂᐊᒪᑕ ᑎᑎᒐᓂᐊᕗᓂ ᐊᑭᓕᒍᑎᓴᓂ ᑐᓯᐊᕕᓴᒧᑦ.

The missionaries brought it and Pootagook had them put it over at the end of the bay where the children wouldn't get at it. He told them to put it there. Pootagook and other Eskimos led the services but, later, a clergyman came and lived here for a time. The women in Cape Dorset sewed sealskin cushions and we also embroidered hangings for the altar. Many women embroidered birds and seals and other animals in bright colours on small

ᐊᔪᑭᑐᐃᕗᐅᑉ ᓂᐅᕕᐊᑎᓕᐅᓯᒪᕗᒐ ᑕᐃᒪ ᐳᑐᓕᐅᑉ ᐃᓕᕗᑯᓕ ᐅᓯᒪᕗᕆ ᐃᒪᐅᑉ ᐃᓯᐊᓄ ᑕᐃᑲᓂ ᐱᐊᕋᓄ ᐅᐃᕕᓴᑕᐅᓂᐊᕆᒪ ᐅᑲᐅᑎᓕᐅᓯᒪᕗᕆ ᑕᐃᑯᒐᑕᐅᑯᓯᒍ. ᐳᑐᓕ ᐊᓯᕆᓗ ᐃᓄᐃᑦ ᑐᓯᐊᑎᓯᕗᐅᕙᓕᐅᑐ ᐃᓚ ᓯᐊᕈ ᐊᔪᑭᑐᐃᕗ ᑎᑭᓕᐅᓯᓇᔪᒃ ᑕᒪᓂᓕᑐ ᐊᑯᓂᐊᓗ. ᐊᒃᓇᐃᑦ ᑭᒐᒥᐅ ᒥᓯᓕᐅᓯᒪᔪ ᓇᓯᐅᑉ ᑭᓯᕆᓂ ᐊᑎᑎᓂ ᑕᐃᒪᓗᑕᐅ ᑕᓯᑐᐃᓕᐅᓯᒪᒥᔪᒍ ᑲᒐᑕᔪᓴᓂ ᑐᓯᐊᕕᐅᑉ ᐃᒥᕕᒐᓂ. ᐊᒥᓯᑦ ᐊᒃᓇᐄᑦ ᑕᒃᓴᓕᐅᓕᐅᓯᒪᔪᑦ ᑯᐸᓄᐊᒍᐊᓂ ᐊᒪᓗ ᓇᓯᒍᐊᓂ ᐊᓯᕆᓂᓗ ᐅᒪᔪᓂ ᓂᑕᓕᑎᑎᓗᕆ

Waiting.
Felt pen, 1970

ᐅᑕᕿᕐᖦ
ᐊᒪᓚᒍ ᐊᒡᐅᑎᒍᑦ ᑎᑎᕐᒪ, 1970

The old life was hard – but it
was happy.
Felt pen, ca. 1967

ᐃᓄᕈᑐᖦ ᐊᒡᐱᓇᓱᐊᕐᓇ ᑡᐊᑡᐸᒡᐊᑐ
ᒍᖦ ᐊᒪᒍᓐ ᑎᑎᕐᒪ,
1967 ᐅᓄᒍ

squares of cloth. But we did much more embroidery than
is there in the church today. What happened to it? Well,
we think one of the missionaries' wives stole some of it.
When all the squares were sewn together they looked
very nice.

I have heard that they like my drawings in the south and
I am grateful and happy about it. Nowadays, when very
special people arrive on the plane to visit the Co-op,
I am always invited. I am usually very shy but often they
shake hands. Last week a very important minister was
here from Ottawa and they gave him the stone which was
made from one of my drawings. It was a sealskin boat
I did last winter.

To make prints is not easy. You must think first and this
is hard to do. But I am happy doing the prints. After my
husband died I felt very alone and unwanted; making prints
is what has made me happiest since he died. I am going
to keep on doing them until they tell me to stop. If no

ᑕᖦᕼᒥ ᒥᕐᕙᓄ ᕸᓄᑐᒍᕊ ᑳᓄᑕᓂ. ᐃᑯ ᐊᒥᕐᑳᓄᖦ
ᑕᖦᕊᑐᐃᓚᐅᕐᒪᕐᓄᑦ ᐱᑕᖦᕊᐊᒐᐃᑐ ᑐᕐᐊᒪᒥ ᒪᓗ. ᑳᐃᓪ
ᓎᖦ? ᑕᒪ ᐊᕊᕐᒍᐃᕥ ᐃᑕᒪ ᓄᑳᒪᓄ ᑎᑤᐸᓇᐅᕊᑐᕊᕥ
ᐃᑕᕐᔦ. ᐃᓄᒪᓐ ᕸᓄᕥ ᒥᕐᕈᒪᓚᐅᑐᐊᒪᕐᖦ ᑳᑎᒥᕊᑎᖦ
ᐱᐅᕐᑳᓄᐅᑐᕐᒪᕊᔦ.

ᑐᕊᐅᑐᒪ ᑎᑎᕈᕊᓗᖦ ᐱᐅᕊᕐᐅᕊᐊᕐᔦ ᑳᓄᕊ ᓄᓇᒥ,
ᓐᕥᕊᑐᒪ ᕼᐊᐊᕊᓚᓕ ᑕᕣᐊ ᒥᕸᓄ. ᓚᒪᐅᑐᐊᕊ, ᐊᒪᕊᑳᓐᑎᖦ
ᓐᕡᒪᕥ ᑳᓄᕊᕣᕐ ᓄᐅᕥᕊᑎ ᕣᕣᐊᕊᒍᐊ, ᑳᐃᐅᕊᐅᕸᕐᓄᕊᕨᕣ
ᐊᖦᕐᕣᓚ ᑳᒍᕊᕊᕣᕨᕣ ᐃᑯ ᕼᐊᒍᕣᑐᔦ. ᕳᕐᕝᐊᕈᕨᐅᑳᑐᕣᒍ
ᐊᒪᕊᑳᓐᑎ ᑕᕣᓕᑳᐅᕊᐊᕊ ᐊᒍᕣᒥ ᕳᓪᓇ ᑕᐊᒪᕊ ᐅᕸᕣᕝᖦ
ᐊᐊᐅᑕᐅᑳᕊᐅᑐᖦ ᐊᕊᕳᑕᐊᓄᒥ ᑎᑎᕈᕊᕣᕳ ᐃᑕᓚᓇᒥ. ᓇᕊᐅᕥ
ᕳᕊᕈᓚᕥᕣᕳ ᐅᒪᕊᐊ ᑎᑎᕈᕊᓄᑕᐅᑳᕊᕣᕳ ᐊᖦᖦ.

ᑎᑎᕈᕊᓐᑎᐊᕼᕼ ᐱᑐᐃᓄᕳᕥᕣᒍ. ᐊᕊᕣᒥᐊᕳᓇᑐ ᐊᕣᓚ ᑕᕳ ᑕᕊᕐ
ᐱᕥᕥᐊᕳᕊᕊᓚᓄ. ᐃᑯ ᕣᐊᐊᕊᕊᑐᓚ ᑎᑎᕈᕊᕳᕥᑐᕊᐊᕼᖦ. ᐅᕣᒪ
ᑐᑯᓚᕼᑎᒍᒍ ᐃᕳᐊᕊᓚᓇᕐᐅᑐᓪᓄᕨᒪᒥ ᐃᓄᐅᕊᕣᑎᓄᕥᒥᖦᓚᓄ, ᑎᑎᕈᕊᕳᕊᐊᕨᑎ
ᒪ ᕼᐊᐊᕊᓐᑕᕊᐊᐅᓄᐊᑐᐅᕊᓚᓄᕊᑐᓚᕊᕨᕣ ᑕᕳᒪᕣ ᐅᕣᒪ ᑐᑯᕊᐅᕊᕥ.

one tells me to stop, I shall make them as long as I am well.
If I can, I'll make them even after I am dead.

My son, Kumwartok, wants me to do some drawings to put
around the house. But I think I will probably do some and
take them to the Co-op.

ᓐᓄᖕᕆᐊᓕᔪᒪᑦ ᓄᒃᑯᖕᐅᕆᓂᒪᑦᖔᓂ. ᐸᒍᐃᐊᒍ ᓄᓄᒃᑯᖕ
ᐅᕿᒍᒪ, ᓐᓄᖕᔪ ᐃᐊᓕᔪᒪᑦ ᑲᓄᐃᕆᓂᒪᓂ. ᒍᐊᒍᒪ.

ᐃᖅᓂᒪ ᒍᓪᐊᑐ ᓐᓄᖕᒍᔅᑎᐊᑐ ᐅᕝᓂ ᐃᒍᓂ ᑲᒪᑕᖔᓂ.
ᐃᓕ ᓐᓄᖕᑲᒍᑐᒪ ᓐᓄᖕᑕᒃ ᒍᐅᐊᖕᒍᑐᐃᐊᓕᑯᕿᕆ.